INTEROCEPTION
AND REGULATION

by the same author

**The Parents' Practical Guide to Resilience for Preteens
and Teenagers on the Autism Spectrum**
Jeanette Purkis and Emma Goodall
ISBN 978 1 78592 275 6
eISBN 978 1 78450 575 2

**The Parents' Practical Guide to Resilience for
Children aged 2–10 on the Autism Spectrum**
Jeanette Purkis and Emma Goodall
ISBN 978 1 78592 274 9
eISBN 978 1 78450 574 5

The Guide to Good Mental Health on the Autism Spectrum
Jeanette Purkis, Emma Goodall and Jane Nugent
Forewords by Wenn Lawson and Kirsty Dempster-Rivett
ISBN 978 1 84905 670 0
eISBN 978 1 78450 195 2

The Autism Spectrum Guide to Sexuality and Relationships
Understand Yourself and Make Choices that are Right for You
Dr Emma Goodall
Forewords by Wenn Lawson and Jeanette Purkis
ISBN 978 1 84905 705 9
eISBN 978 1 78450 226 3

INTEROCEPTION and REGULATION

Teaching Skills of Body Awareness and Supporting Connection with Others

Emma Goodall
and **Charlotte Brownlow**

Foreword by Wenn Lawson

Jessica Kingsley Publishers
London and Philadelphia

First published in Great Britain in 2022 by Jessica Kingsley Publishers
An imprint of Hodder & Stoughton Ltd
An Hachette Company

1

A CIP catalogue record for this title is available from the
British Library and the Library of Congress

ISBN 978 1 78775 728 8
eISBN 978 1 78775 729 5

Printed and bound in Great Britain by TJ Books Limited, Padstow, Cornwall

Jessica Kingsley Publishers' policy is to use papers that are natural, renewable
and recyclable products and made from wood grown in sustainable
forests. The logging and manufacturing processes are expected to conform
to the environmental regulations of the country of origin.

Jessica Kingsley Publishers
Carmelite House
50 Victoria Embankment
London EC4Y 0DZ

www.jkp.com

This book is dedicated to all of the children and adults who we have worked with over the years who have taught us so much about their experience of interoception. It is through these shared experiences that we can all learn a little more about ourselves. In particular, the young people who told Emma that doing interoception activities had enabled them to control their anger, rather than their anger controlling them, were the spark that lit Emma's passion to share her learnings about interoception.

Contents

Foreword

E MMA AND CHARLOTTE'S BOOK couldn't have come at a better time. I hear so much about 'challenging behaviour' and the costs to society of housing and providing for individuals in our justice systems and other institutions. I also have families and teachers writing to me to ask how to handle their son, daughter, or student's 'challenging behaviours' because schools and families are not coping and have no idea what to do with these individuals. So many get put on 'Good Behaviour Bonds' or end up being expelled from schools and continue to act out in their homes or on the streets.

As the authors of this book so beautifully point out, without interoceptive awareness one cannot have interoceptive accuracy. So, while we may get upset, disappointed, or even angry about another's behaviour, we must first ask ourselves if that individual realizes they have caused us discomfort? It might be they have no awareness of 'self' or of 'other'.

I once had a loving grandmother in the audience of a talk I was giving on autism and sensory issues. She told me how upsetting it was to have her eight-year-old autistic granddaughter, who was upset about something, run away from her 'comforting' arms. I tried to explain to this lady that her granddaughter wasn't rejecting her; it was all that came with her that she was rejecting...it was overwhelming her granddaughter. Her autistic granddaughter wasn't able to separate her grandmother's comforting embrace from the overwhelming 'noise' of her voice, her hair, her clothing, and so on. First, her granddaughter needed to hear acknowledgement of her distress, then she needed guidance as to where she could safely 'sit' for some quiet moments, where she could allow her nervous system to settle so she could accept 'comfort' and not experience it as excruciating. Too often children hear us say things like 'It's OK, no need to be upset, Grannie's here'. Such words are not helpful because they negate a child's experience of being upset and they don't provide a solution that is going to help remedy their responses.

Emma and Charlotte's book will take you on a journey and help you to identify the qualities of your eighth sense, what they each mean and how to support their connection with your emotions. It's only once we can do this that we are able to self-regulate, self-soothe, and self-acknowledge. In being able to do these things for ourselves, we can recognize them in others and can become more resilient, less judgmental, and more compassionate. As human beings we are governed by our neuroception or the basic survival instincts passed down throughout the generations; it's in our DNA. However, genetics don't rule the roost on their own. Generational trauma, passed down and across the generations within cellular memory, is also a component that dictates our emotional states. Emma and Charlotte clearly illustrate this dynamic and speak to those potential triggers that tip the scales into the various depths we find ourselves overtaken by.

Neuroception is the autonomic, unconscious sense that warns the body of danger (see Porges, 2004). It allows a person to connect to the five Fs (Fear, Flight, Freeze, Fight, and Fawn). In autism and various cousins, however, this system will be skewed, meaning we are primed for anxiety and possible hypervigilance, hypovigilance, or disconnection to self and others around us.

Neuroception works with our interoceptive self. Interoception is a sense like our other senses, but it lets us connect to our internal world (e.g. heart rate, breathing, pain, temperature, appetite, thirst, sexual desire, etc.), rather than the external world (e.g. sight, hearing, touch, taste, smell, vestibular, etc.). Interoception is a sense that is often neglected, though, not just in terms of academic research; as human beings, we may not realize how important interoception is. Emma and Charlotte take us on a journey of discovery, allowing us to appreciate how to 'wake up' to our eighth sense, recognize this system, and use it to our advantage.

They show us the reasons we need a good interoceptive sense that is fine-tuned; otherwise, we may not have access to 'self-regulation' of our emotions. In taking the time to understand both neuroception and interoception, and how these impact our differing processing systems (which are different according to whether you are part of the non-autistic population or the autistic population), we will be equipping ourselves for the daily demands of human existence. Being neurodiverse means different things to different people, but it is part and parcel of being human. Of course, we are all neurodiverse – after all, neurodiversity is to the brain and nervous system what bio-diversity is to the animals and plants of planet earth. But if you operate from an autistic cognitive style, you will have a brain that works with single attention or monotropism. Therefore, for us it's doubly important to take time and to explore what remediation is needed to build appropriate connection to our fuller 'selves' that contributes to uncovering identity, personality, and our total 'self-concept'.

As autistic individuals, we may exhibit behaviours that appear challenging and unreasonable to outside observers. At times, such behaviours have been linked to a lack of empathy, to being difficult, and to not appreciating concepts associated with theory of mind (ToM – knowing others have their own thoughts, feelings, and ideas that may be different from one's own). For example, many autistic individuals find it difficult to maintain eye contact and identify emotions of self or others, and struggle to generalize various concepts (yours, mine, then, later, and so on). But this inability to attend to several things simultaneously has been misinterpreted as poor ToM. However, these two concepts are vastly different, as Emma and Charlotte rightly point out. We each need to recognize the signs before we can read them. Once we can recognize them, we can read them and act upon them. If, however, we are not picking up on the signs, we cannot act on their message. The fact that we can act once we notice and understand what they mean says we don't lack ToM; we simply aren't recognizing or connecting to the signs. If we lacked ToM, it wouldn't matter if we connected to an understanding of self or other; we just wouldn't 'get it'. Emma and Charlotte clearly offer the right signposts to build connection, once again debunking the myth of a lack of ToM in autism.

Interoception (the conscious connection to what's happening inside ourselves, e.g. our heart rate, feelings of hunger, thirst, needing to empty our bladder, anger, whether we are hot, cold, and so on) is also required for the cognitive development of object permanence (knowing an object/person/place continues to exist even when you cannot see it). For example, the sun remains in the sky even when it's behind the clouds. Without interoception, it's much harder to regulate emotions and connect to the bigger picture that tells us what we or others might need. It's also harder to connect to the notion of object permanence.

Interoception and object permanence require individuals to attend to multiple stimuli. For autistics, this is difficult. In regard to object permanence, whether the object is in view or hidden from view, autistic individuals may discern details but not the wider context. For example, two autistic students might know their drink bottles are in their lunch bag, even when they can't see them, but they don't seem to know that Mummy is still there, just not within their view. How is it they know one concept, but not the other? For object permanence and interoception to develop, individuals must make connections and 'notice' what is happening within their body as well as outside of themselves. It is thought that autism, due to a lack of 'big picture' thinking which requires a full range of cognitive and sensorimotor skills to work synchronously within the brain, makes it very difficult to notice things inside and outside of ourselves at the same time. This can be a barrier for individuals to determine 'Where/how am I?' and 'Where is it?' especially with regard to object permanence.

Neuroplasticity describes the way to change an individual's cognitive skills by intentionally changing the brain by creating new neural connections. Intentional change occurs through repeated exposure to novel/new tasks that strengthen neural connections involved in a range of cognitive processes such as visual, auditory, and speed processing, short-term and long-term memory, attention, logic, and reasoning. Emma and Charlotte paint the picture for us of why an interoception exercise programme needs to be repeated three or more times a day.

However, for learning to take place, the individual must be 'attending', and we need to encourage them to find ways of noticing. This might be through the use of an individual's passion. Whatever is most interesting for the autistic individual will win their single point of focus/attention. This single focus is a useful strategy. For example, if the individual is most interested in a Disney princess doll, then the Disney princess doll must be incorporated into the novel task in order to capture the individual's interest and attention, enabling them to learn a novel/new task or skill. Disney characters, Lego models, video games (such as Sims video games), comic-strip stories based upon superheroes, dinosaurs, role playing, and so on are all ideal motivators that can be used to initiate interest across the broader concepts of object permanence, if within an individual's existing passion. With the exercise programmes Emma and Charlotte write about, if you incorporate an individual's passion, it will make the programme even more attractive.

Being able to grasp why some behaviour is so challenging, what causes this, and how to remedy it is vitally important. Being able to understand connections to interoception and object permanence in autistics builds confidence in us as individuals, our families, carers, teachers, and those clinicians who support us. It is a myth that autistics lack empathy. Exploring ways and means to build concepts that relieve fear and anxiety in autistic individuals changes lives for the better. Appreciating the differences between a fully developed sense of interoception and object permanence when compared with ToM issues not only changes perceptions but enables appropriate support.

Within the following pages of Emma and Charlotte's book, you will read all about our eighth sense, why it's so important to understand this sense, and how you can help to build this sense, either for yourself or by co-regulation as you work to support others. I can only hope you get as much from this book as I have and that you use it to dive in and out of as you explore answers to unlocking the reasons and the remedies for connections to self and to others.

Dr. Wenn Lawson (PhD) CPsychol AFBPsS MAPS

CHAPTER 1

What Is Interoception?

THERE ARE SOME THINGS that many of us take for granted in terms of our knowledge and understanding, such as how we know we are hot or hungry, or need to go to the toilet. But how do we know these things and why do some people struggle to recognize them? Describing these feelings accurately can be difficult. Also, we sometimes don't interpret the signals accurately, and as a result we commonly hear of people being referred to as 'hangry' or 'over-tired', suggesting that we might not always recognize some of the core internal cues in time before they begin to affect our outward behaviours. Misinterpretations of internal bodily states are common in children, but it is not only children who sometimes misread or overlook internal cues; this can happen for adults as well. The ability to recognize our internal cues is referred to as *interoception*. This book is designed to introduce you to the concept of interoception and its importance and impact on a range of behaviours, while keeping a practical focus on what you as a parent, carer, or professional might do to support interoceptive abilities in the people that you love, support, or teach.

The book is based on our experiences as researchers exploring the phenomenon of interoception, but we will also share some of our own experiences of our own interoceptive engagement. As such, it will be a mixture of looking at the current literature and what we know from our own and others' research about the concept of interoception and its development, and what happens when the reading of our body signals doesn't quite go right, and exploring what can be done to foster interoceptive skills in ourselves and others, and why this is useful.

The book will begin with this chapter, Chapter 1, exploring what interoception is, summarizing research and understanding of concepts to date, and reflecting on what interoception means in terms of connection to self. Chapter 2 will focus on the development of interoceptive abilities and consider these within the broader context of development and learning. Chapter 3 will explore what happens when interoceptive abilities are challenging for a person and how these difficulties might be identified and supported. Building on the literature introduced in Chapters 1, 2, and 3, the remaining chapters will provide practical strategies to manage feelings and emotions and support individuals in 'tuning in' to themselves. However, before we engage with the practical and applied activities that might support interoception, we must first understand what interoception is and how it is conceptualized both in terms of theory and current research that seeks to assess the impacts of interventions based on research.

MANAGING THE SELF

Emma first became interested in interoception following requests from schools she worked with, asking for help in supporting students to self-manage and self-regulate. The consequences for schools of students not being able to do this effectively was frequently resulting in poor engagement with learning. Delays or difficulties with self-management and self-regulation in children and young people therefore come with a high cost to those individuals themselves, as well as their peers, families, and involved professionals (Füstös *et al.*, 2012; Moffitt, Poulton, & Caspi, 2013; Nigg, 2017; Slutske *et al.*, 2012). The concept of self-management refers to ongoing, dynamic, and adaptive behaviours, which are made as responses to internal states relating to biological homeostasis needs within the body. In contrast, self-regulation refers to the individual's ability to control and helpfully express their own social-emotional needs and wants, thoughts, emotions, and actions (Heatherton & Tice, 1994). Conceptually, there is a distinction between self-management and self-regulation based in responses to internal states relating to biological homeostasis needs, but, practically, self-regulatory behaviours can arise from self-management needs. For example, Nigg (2017) highlighted that poor self-regulation arising from self-management demands is implicated in increased mental health difficulties, increased physical ill-health, and lower life outcomes for children, which impacts social and academic outcomes.

The wide-ranging negative impact of poor self-regulation means that it is important to support families, professionals, and the education system to improve children's self-regulation effectively, especially as related to self-management needs, which can be among the most pressing demands for self-regulation. Self-regulation enables children to engage in learning activities (Blair & Raver, 2015), and with poor self-regulation comes less engagement in learning and higher rates of internalizing and externalizing (disruptive) behaviours. Therefore, families and educators can struggle to manage children and young people who are highly dysregulated and unable to self-regulate. Interoception is thought to be crucial to individuals self-managing their behaviour, reducing the likelihood of dysregulated behaviour occurring and increasing the effectiveness of both self-regulation and co-regulation. Co-regulation is where someone else provides the strategies and supports for an individual to be able to manage and become calmer rather than more dysregulated.

INTEROCEPTION: THE EIGHTH SENSE

Interoception is sometimes referred to as somatic awareness or somatic interoceptive awareness (Kanbara & Fukunaga, 2016), and is colloquially known as the eighth sense (Mahler, 2016), with the other seven being sight, hearing, taste, smell, touch, proprioception, and vestibular (Lynch & Simpson, 2004). While most people are familiar with sight, hearing, taste, smell, and touch, the vestibular and proprioception senses are less well known and are focused on the awareness of the whole body. Vestibular refers to our sense of balance, which is governed by the inner ear, and proprioception refers to the sense of where our body is placed in space – for example, where our head ends and space starts – which is useful to prevent us banging our heads on overhanging objects. Theoretically, interoception can be described as mindful body awareness, as it is the conscious perception (mindful) of internal body signals (body awareness).

Interoception is therefore the awareness of the physiological state of the body, possibly originating in the visceral organs. Interoception at a physiological and psychological level is implicated in maintaining homeostasis and regulating emotions (Badoud & Tsakiris, 2017). Much like the other senses, interoception has at least two components: interoceptive awareness and interoceptive accuracy (Calì et al., 2015). Interoceptive awareness refers to metacognitive abilities relating to a person's own bodily performance (Garfinkel et al., 2016); that is to say, the individual is aware of their internal body signals in relation to the body's needs (for homeostasis) and wants (emotions). Researchers have currently referenced interoceptive accuracy solely in relation to heartbeat detection, rather than more generally as accurate perception of the internal body signals. For example, Garfinkel et al. (2016) defined interoceptive accuracy as 'performance on objective behavioural tests of heartbeat detection' (p.65). While the facets explain different aspects of interoception, some argue there is no significant correlation between each of them, suggesting that interoception is not a single entity, but a concept with multiple dimensions (Meessen *et al.*, 2016). This would seem to make sense given the range of recognitions that an individual must engage with and accurately label in order to maintain a sense of balance within the body. Most of these happen at an unconscious level – for example, we are not always aware of our own heartbeat until we focus our attention on this.

Interoceptive awareness can therefore be broadly defined as the conscious perception of an internal bodily state such as one's heart beating and the lungs inhaling and exhaling air. This definition can also apply to mindful body awareness, the conscious noticing in the present moment of body signals. These senses, when grouped together, are related to emotional experiences – for example, when we are tired, we will be experiencing several internal body signals that, when grouped together, signal 'tired'. However, research has indicated that not all of us have the same abilities when it comes to recognizing our own body's signals. Awareness of physiological internal body cues has been shown to be altered in individuals who are affected by trauma, including intergenerational trauma, and neurodevelopmental disabilities including autism (Mahler, 2016; Schauder *et al.*, 2015). This is something that we will come back to in more detail in Chapter 3. However, what is common to us all is a background of the human species' survival instinct, including our biological need for and drive towards homeostasis, and with this in mind, interoceptive awareness can be broadly split into three categories:

- the ability to notice internal body signals (Craig, 2002)
- the ability to notice and interpret collections of body signals as emotions and feelings (Craig, 2009)

- the ability to notice external signals and interpret the impact these will have on the body (Craig, 2009).

On a neuroanatomical level, interoception has mostly been linked to two key cortical areas: the insular cortex (IC) and the anterior cingulate cortex (ACC) (Badoud & Tsakiris, 2017). The insular cortex is thought to be the 'hub' of interoception, integrating physiological and emotional perception, while the ACC is also implicated in the perception of interoceptive signals (Couto *et al.*, 2015). However, there is evidence to suggest that the IC and ACC are not the only areas involved in interoception, and that the medial temporal lobe (MTL) is also critical in this sense. Berriman and colleagues' (2016) animal lesion study supported this theory when it discovered that removal of the hippocampus was followed by dysregulation of hunger and satiety.

In her previous work, Emma created a visual depiction of the theoretical way the combination of these categories of interoceptive awareness enables people to respond to their internal body signals and therefore, in effect, understand themselves and develop the skills to self-regulate and self-manage (Figure 1.1).

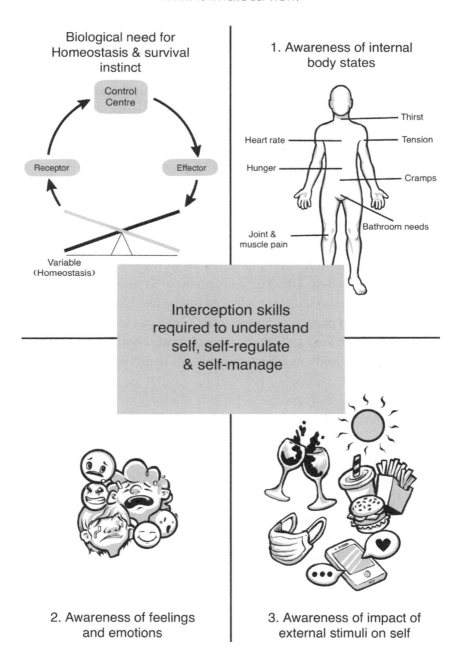

SELF-REGULATION VS. SELF-MANAGEMENT

Füstös and colleagues (2012) suggested that self-regulation of emotions is reliant on both attention to and awareness of one's emotional state, which could be linked to or interpreted as interoception. Self-regulation is commonly understood as the moderation or control of emotions and behaviour in order to follow social norms in a particular context. This is sometimes referred to as self-control. Self-management, on the other hand, is related to the control or actioning of behaviours in order to fulfil biological needs, usually in accordance with a drive to return to homeostasis (Craig, 2007). Self-management behaviours include drinking water when thirsty or putting a sweater on when cold. Self-management is more obviously linked to homeostasis, as evidenced by the need for our bodies to be within a particular temperature range and to have energy input through food and output through waste elimination, or by energy usage and muscle movement within given parameters.

THE IMPORTANCE OF INTEROCEPTIVE MASTERY

Interoception skills are required for a range of basic and more advanced functions that we as individuals need to engage with, such as knowing when to go to the toilet, being aware that you are becoming angry or upset, and being able to manage our emotions proactively. Children and young people who have not yet developed interoception skills struggle not only with their own emotions (Brewer, Cook, & Bird, 2016) but also with social interactions and sometimes just being around others (Goodall *et al.*, 2019). However, despite these indications of links, there is a significant gap in the literature concerning understandings of the relationship between interoception and emotional regulation, with most research only looking at how interventions involving interoception are effective in ameliorating a range of mental ill-health symptoms (Khoury, Lutz, & Schuman-Olivier, 2018). Furman and colleagues (2013), for example, have found that altered interoception in adults with major depression impacted the participants' ability to feel positive as well as their ability to make decisions based on interoceptive signals. Also, in her previous work, Emma has researched the impact of teaching interoception on improving self-regulation. Generally, however, there is a dearth of research on the impact of altered interoception on developing or improving interpersonal difficulties, self-regulation, social anxiety, or other behaviours in adults or children. It seems likely that children and young people with well-developed interoception are able to use both logic and emotions to respond to their environment, whereas those without tend to rely solely on logic and have to carefully think through their possible responses to each situation. This may be familiar to many autistic individuals who tend to rely more on logic than emotions. Constantly having to think through each situation can be extremely tiring and contribute to overload, shutdown, meltdowns, anxiety, and depression. It would therefore seem that being able to accurately recognize and read your own bodily signals has far-reaching effects both in the management of self and also the effective engagement with others.

Emotions and actions are understood to have a contextual element, in that individuals express emotions or carry out actions in response to their thoughts and/or their experience of the context around them (Wilutzky, 2015). Indeed, Grecucci, Koch, and Rumiati (2011) found that emotions can also impact imitative actions (e.g. if someone waves their hands excitedly, people around are more likely to wave excitedly back). Due to its perceived importance, Goleman (1995) described emotional and behavioural self-regulation as top-level skills in an emotional intelligence hierarchy. Goleman suggested that emotional intelligence, sometimes known as social intelligence, is composed of three skill sets: emotional skills, cognitive skills, and behaviour skills. When these theories are looked at in conjunction with metacognition, thinking about thinking (Moses & Baird, 1999; Wellman, 1985), the key role of interoception can be identified.

TWO COMPONENTS: AWARENESS AND ACCURACY

Much like the other senses, interoception has at least two components: interoceptive awareness and interoceptive accuracy (Calì *et al.*, 2015). We would argue that interoception can also be described as mindful body awareness, as it is the conscious perception (mindful) of internal body signals (body awareness). Mindfulness is a broad term, used in popular culture in a variety of ways. As a lifestyle concept, mindfulness means to pay attention on purpose (Sher, 2016), in the present moment, and non-judgmentally, whereas as a spiritual concept, mindfulness can be used to mean being present and aware (Fox Lee, 2019). In this book, we take mindful body awareness rather than mindfulness as the focus. For us, mindful body awareness is purposeful attention in the present moment that is focused on changes and sensations within the body or self (interoception). This focused attention should guide the plasticity of the brain to create and strengthen interoceptive-aware brain connections, as per the findings of Ahissar and colleagues (2009). Someone skilled at mindful body awareness can, for example, tell when their heartbeat is signalling fear versus excitement because they can notice and recognize or identify all the other internal bodily signals that they are experiencing, which help them to process and respond to their overall emotional state. On a more basic level, interoception enables people to know when they are hungry, thirsty, tired, etc., all of which are necessary precursors to positive development and self-regulation.

However, this system of recognition is not always accurate and recognized. Research conducted by Goodall (2020) reported that some children and young people seemingly did not notice they were angry until they were enraged, or notice thirst until they were dehydrated. This lack of connection to self could be explained by either poor interoceptive accuracy or, more likely, poor interoceptive awareness. The link between interoceptive awareness and mindfulness, in relation to sense of self, can be found in research on the embodied sense of self (Cook-Cottone, 2015; Craig, 2003, 2009; Damasio, 1999). Damasio (1999) proposed that human awareness and experience of emotional feelings are reliant on neural states that represent internal body signals, with collections of body signals evoking feeling states/emotions that influence both cognition and behaviour. If, for example, individuals were not noticing their emotional states, this would be why they didn't do anything about emerging emotional states, and once individuals became aware of their heightened emotional state, it was often too late to do anything about it as they were in sympathetic nervous system overload/survival mode (Goodall, 2019).

VISUALIZING THE THEORETICAL LINKS

So far we have focused on the theory behind interoception, with suggestions as to how this may influence an individual's behaviour. One way of making sense of these theories and their translation into observable behaviours is shown in Figure 1.2. This visualization draws on Siegel's (2010) 'hand model of the brain', extending the model beyond visible behaviours to demonstrate that connecting with your internal body signals is crucial to being able to recognize and accurately interpret your 'self' in order to engage in mindful body awareness – or interoception.

In Siegel's model, the middle two fingernails represent the mindfulness part of the brain, which can only be engaged when the fist is fully closed and the 'thinking cap of the brain' is engaged. Theoretically, engaging in mindful body awareness, or interoception, activities will engage the mindfulness part of the brain, leading to the thinking cap of the brain also being engaged and the parasympathetic nervous system being activated, which would enable an individual, neurologically and biologically, to 'calm down', making self-regulation both possible and more likely to happen. When individuals are in sympathetic nervous system overload, otherwise known as survival mode, they cannot self-regulate their emotions as the brain's survival instinct takes over (Siegel, 2010). In effect, in survival mode, it is not the individual that is in control of their behaviour but their survival instinct, which is designed to keep the individual alive and as safe as possible. Figure 1.2 draws on Siegel's theory to combine the thinking cap of the brain, emotional brain, and survival/reptile brain from Siegel's hand model of the brain with levels of autonomic nervous system (ANS) activity. This illustrates how the two branches of the ANS, the sympathetic nervous system (SNS) and parasympathetic nervous system (PNS), can affect the brain, resulting in changes in behavioural 'zones' – learning zone, big emotions, and survival zone. In this model, as mentioned above, individuals are unable to control their behaviours or regulate their emotions in the panic zone, as their survival instinct has overtaken conscious thought, resulting in behaviours that can be challenging to themselves and/or others. Interoception enables people to self-regulate as they know when they are heading towards big emotions or their panic zone, enabling them to do something to prevent themselves from entering big emotions or the panic zone.

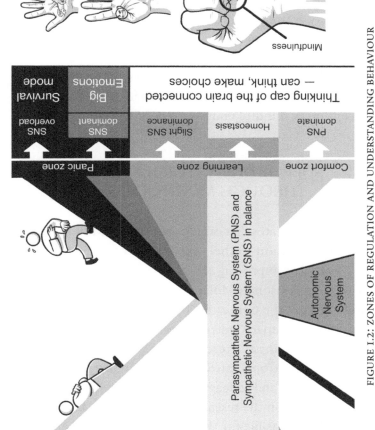

FIGURE 1.2: ZONES OF REGULATION AND UNDERSTANDING BEHAVIOUR

Source: Goodall et al, 2019

In interpreting Figure 1.2, it is clear that a person cannot experience mindfulness without being in the learning zone, implying that when being mindful, the PNS is activated and the person is neurologically calmed. Pascoe and Crewther (2017) found that meditation activates the PNS, reducing anxiety symptomology, while Zitron and Gao (2017) reported that mindfulness activates the PNS. We can therefore deduce that engaging in mindful body awareness (interoception) activities can activate the PNS and thereby neurologically calms an individual. This was confirmed by the adults, children, and young people that Emma worked with over the last five years, who talked about feeling calmer and more in control of themselves after doing interoception or mindful body awareness activities.

SUPPORTING INTEROCEPTION THROUGH MINDFULNESS

Research demonstrates that mindfulness leads to improvement for people in relation to their experience of depression and anxiety, as well as improving self-compassion and compassion for others (e.g. Idusohan-Moizer *et al.*, 2015). In a pilot study, researchers from the Center for Investigating Healthy Minds (CIHM) at the Waisman Center, University of Wisconsin-Madison, taught mindfulness to teachers, children, and young people in the Madison Metropolitan School District. In evaluating this programme, Flook and colleagues (2015) reported that children and young people in the research group said they felt more in control and responsible for their actions. An explanation for this could be as per Siegel's (2010) hand model of the brain, that individuals are not in control of their actions when they are in 'big emotions or panic zone' and mindfulness can only occur when the thinking cap of the brain, the neocortex, is connected and active. Their teachers suggested that the children and young people in this mindfulness training research made fewer errors while demonstrating improved use of strategy in problem-solving tasks involving working memory and improved emotion regulation. The CIHM also looked at preschools and teaching kindness and compassion through mindfulness, and found that these children and young people showed greater improvements in social competence as well as higher levels of learning, health, and social-emotional development, whereas the control group exhibited more selfish behaviour over time (Flook *et al.*, 2015). This suggests that it may be possible to teach emotional and behavioural self-regulation through mindful body awareness/interoception activities.

Indeed, recent work by Emma has demonstrated that, as previously suggested by researchers and practitioners such as Mahler (2016) and van der Kolk (2014), it is practical and effective to implement the teaching of interoceptive skills to facilitate improvements in both interoceptive awareness and accuracy. What Emma further found, however, was that these interoceptive skills had a positive impact on emotional and/ or behavioural self-regulation or social-emotional confidence and competency. In a year-long pilot interoception programme with 11 schools in South Australia, Emma's findings demonstrated a reduction in reported behavioural consequences across the schools, with qualitative findings detailing the impacts of learning interoceptive techniques for individuals and their own perceptions of their behaviours (Goodall, 2021). This work clearly identifies not only the need to teach interoception but also the clear impacts on students' abilities to regulate their own behaviours, enabling better engagement with learning – a key issue outlined by teachers to Emma prior to the research.

CHAPTER SUMMARY

What is clear from the knowledge that we currently have is that interoception seems to play a key role in a range of experiences for individuals, both in terms of physiological responses and emotional experiences. Understanding how individuals typically develop interoceptive mastery will be the focus of the next chapter, which will help us to better understand how we can support those who are still honing their interoceptive skills.

CHAPTER 2

The Development of Interoceptive Abilities in Children

A S WE SAW IN CHAPTER 1, mastery of our own interoceptive abilities, and its importance for allowing us to recognize our own internal bodily signals, is central to managing our feelings, emotions, and actions. What we would like to focus on in this chapter is how this skill develops. This is not a simple task and most certainly does not just happen automatically all of the time, though it can seem like it for people with very good interoception. Think for one minute about your own bodily signals right now. How are you feeling? Hungry? Tired? Thirsty? Does your back ache? How do you know the answer to these things? Trying to find the words to describe feelings such as hunger and pain can be tricky, and we know, of course, from being 'hangry' or emotional eating that we can sometimes mix up our interpretations of our own bodily signals! Given this can be difficult for adults, how do infants and children manage to develop interoceptive skills, and what helps them to do so?

THE IMPORTANCE OF INTEROCEPTIVE MASTERY FOR CHILDREN

The ability to accurately read our own internal signals and then accurately label and act on these has been shown to have far-reaching implications for children and their engagement with the world. Typically identified developmental milestones such as bladder and bowel control, regulating emotions and behaviour, and managing social interactions all require accurate interoceptive abilities and a good connection and reading of the messages that our own body is trying to tell us. For children and young people, this can have far-reaching implications for key parts of their life, such as educational contexts. Research indicates that fostering the development of self-regulation in early childhood offers the potential to ensure early education is effective for all children (Blair & Raver, 2015). However, in order to manage positive self-regulation, children need to have developed the interoceptive skills to be able to recognize their own feelings and emotions accurately.

Researchers such as Mul and colleagues (2018) highlight the growing body of evidence that points towards links between emotional processing and interoception. They propose that individuals who have a better connection with their own body tend to have a better understanding of both their own emotions and the emotions of others. This, of course, has broader implications for how we understand others and their behaviours and intentions. Interoception would therefore seem to play an important role in both making theories about other people's thinking in terms of their intentions and beliefs (a concept known as theory of mind), and also the display of empathy.

Similarly, researchers Fotopoulou and Tsakiris (2017) also make the connections between the internal self and others, suggesting that interoception may play an important role in self–other boundaries. They argue that internal and external perceptions, or interoceptive and exteroceptive signals, work together to produce not only meaning for an individual but also sense-making for their interactions with others. We don't only see our body from the outside – through a mirror, for example; this is also accompanied by all the internal feelings that other people can't see such as a racing heart and increased pulse rate. Together, these pieces of information tell us how to react to a situation and the role of others within this. Fotopoulou and Tsakiris suggest that people who have lower interoceptive accuracy demonstrate stronger changes in how they view their own bodies following external signals and messages. Therefore, individuals with lower interoceptive skills are more likely to be influenced by the external information they are provided with, which can result in inaccurate interpretations of their own emotions and feelings. For example, someone may assume they are hungry because it is lunchtime, but they may actually be frustrated that they are struggling to do a task or stressed by an unpleasant sensory input.

In order to be fully engaged with all of the information to inform our behavioural choices, we need to be in connection with our own bodies and accurately be able to recognize and identify our own internal signals. Although, at first sight, it would appear to be an internal individual matter, interoception has more far-reaching effects on not only how we see ourselves but how we engage with others. For children, therefore, intero-ceptive abilities are important not only for physiological skills development such as toileting and appropriate choice in clothes to regulate temperature, but also for their social interactions with their peers and adults. The current gap in the research literature is how these very specific skills develop in children and how we continue to adapt and manage these throughout adulthood. We will explore this in the next section.

THE DEVELOPMENT OF INTEROCEPTIVE SKILLS

Although there has been a focus in the research literature concerning the possible biological underpinnings of interoception, the development of interoception and the social influences on this have largely been overlooked. Research that has focused on the role of the social has identified key influences of the relationships that infants and children have with others, specifically adults, and also the part that attachment may play in fostering interoceptive skills.

Researchers Fotopoulou and Tsakiris (2017) argue that there is no reason to assume that either infants or their caregivers would have a clear understanding of the different interoceptive states of the infant or how to act to foster infant understanding of these. This is something that caregivers and infants learn together, resulting in the co-facilitation of interoceptive skills. For example, as Oldroyd, Pasupathi, and Wainryb (2019) highlight, while biological mechanisms induce particular states such as hunger, infants rely heavily on their caregivers to provide cues for understanding the bodily sensations that they are feeling. For example, babies may become fussy when they are hungry but don't connect the feelings they are experiencing with hunger. The caregivers address the fussy behaviour with the provision of milk, and over time the infant begins to connect the internal feelings that they are experiencing with being hungry and the need for food. Similarly, caregivers may initially struggle to understand the cause of the fussy behaviour and try a range of soothing techniques. Over time the caregiver becomes more in tune with their infant's cries and begins to be able to differentiate between cries for food and cries resulting from tiredness. The subtle differences in the cries and more accurate responses from the caregivers further helps to facilitate the differentiation of feelings on the part of the infant. Over time the infant will therefore be able to learn through this process of co-regulation and become more able to recognize cues of hunger or tiredness, and consequently be better able to communicate their feelings and needs.

Researchers propose that this is an ongoing and evolving process, with children's interactions becoming increasingly more complex as they get older. The increasingly complex interactions allow for more sophisticated understandings of their own internal states to be formed, with ongoing support and co-regulation from caregivers. In the previous example of hunger, caregivers responded to cries from a physiological need with the provision of milk. As children grow, the way their parent or caregiver responds to the internal need may be in a more verbal form that allows children to develop the linguistic tools to label accurately what they are feeling. Oldroyd and colleagues use accurate identification and labelling of pain as an example. Think about a child who is running excitedly but trips and falls, resulting in internal sensations of pain, which they may not be able to accurately recognize as such. One parent may respond with 'Ouch! That would have hurt. Let me see,' whereas another parent may respond with 'You're fine! It's all good! Get back up and start again.' Oldroyd and colleagues would argue that the first parent would be better at co-facilitating interoceptive awareness and understanding by drawing joint attention to the incident and clearly and accurately labelling the sensations for the child. The second example would not serve to so clearly identify for the child what their feelings may be, and hence not act to enable clarity in their own internal bodily understandings. While we don't want to make a claim that parents by their actions are solely responsible for the development of interoceptive skills within their children, their behaviours and words as interpreted by their children do appear to help nourish self-understanding in their children.

Another practical example of how parents interact with their children and appear to co-develop the child's interoceptive skills is toilet training. Parents spend time cueing their child on when to go to the toilet or use the potty during toilet training and point out signals to the child – 'You're wiggling/clutching. You need to go to the toilet now.' Children who do not receive this type of feedback may struggle more with toilet training.

THE INFLUENCE OF ATTACHMENT AND EARLY CHILDHOOD TRAUMA

Some researchers have focused on the links between attachment styles and the impacts of early childhood trauma on an individual's interoceptive mastery. Attachments are the connections that individuals form with others, otherwise known as interpersonal relationships, such as loving parent–child relationships or caring teacher–student connections. We know that, generally, children tend to have positive attachments with their caregivers, and we know that these bonds are important in both providing the support needed in childhood and also longer-term effects through to positive relationships in adulthood. However, what about those children who don't have positive attachment experiences or who experience early life adversity? How does this affect their feelings of self and understanding of their own body and its signals?

Oldroyd and colleagues report on the relationship between attachment and interoception, with positive attachments related to more heightened interoceptive abilities. We know that when a child feels securely attached, they have the confidence to use their caregivers as a safe base from which to explore their surroundings and receive cues as to how to manage in unfamiliar contexts. However, we also know that not all children form secure attachments with their caregivers, and as a result some feel the need to become emotionally independent and self-reliant and are reluctant to rely on others for help and support. In contrast, others may become clingy and excessively upset when separated from their caregiver. Oldroyd and colleagues argue that these types of attachments influence the development of interoceptive abilities due to the previously discussed reliance on caregivers for cues to help shape and develop ever-increasing interoceptive understanding. Responses by caregivers, even just 'good enough' ones, are therefore thought to be central in supporting interoceptive development.

Oldroyd and colleagues' research points towards patterns of avoidant attachment styles, where parents or caregivers do not interact with their child much, being linked with lower interoceptive abilities, while those attachments characterized as anxious, such as those where children become highly anxious when their parent or caregiver leaves them, are more likely to have heightened interoceptive abilities. It is thought that either of these extremes can affect individuals in the recognition and management of their own internal cues. It is important to high-light at this point again that we are not suggesting any blame per se on the part of parents and caregivers, but rather we seek to unpack the many different influences on the development of interoception, and the social has been demonstrated to be as impactful as the pure physiological. A complex relationship occurs between the two influences, of course, and these are unique for each individual child.

The experience of adversity in early childhood has been shown to have negative effects on interoceptive abilities in young adulthood. Schaan and colleagues (2019) considered that early life adversity disrupted the development of interoceptive accuracy, which is related to the ability to regulate emotions. The ability to regulate emotions and some techniques you might like to try to support this will be considered in later chap-ters of this book. However, for now, the link between adversity and reduced interoceptive capabilities needs to be unpacked a little further. We know from the previous research that we have introduced in this chapter that interactions with others are crucial in shaping what Fotopoulou and Tsakiris (2017) call the 'mentalization of interoception'. For these researchers, the internal process of interoception derives as much from external cues as it does from internal ones. Young infants who do not have complex experiences and understandings of internal bodily states will be wholly reliant on interactions with others. Disruptions to such interpersonal interactions through trauma and adversity will serve to disrupt the complex understandings of our own body's development, interrupting the 'mentalization of interoception'. It is also possible that a decrease in interoception is one way the brain attempts to protect individuals experiencing ongoing trauma, as it may be less traumatic to 'not feel' the events that are happening in terms of pain and other unpleasant emotions and feelings.

Schaan and colleagues therefore recommend that it is important to help children who have experienced adversity to connect with their body and engage with a range of different feelings that they will experience at different times. Some of these will be short-lived, others more enduring. However, the key point is that they need to be supported in connecting with these feelings, as they have missed out on earlier opportunities of co-facilitation by parents and others. Better differentiation of bodily changes can therefore lead to better perception and management of one's own emotions.

CHAPTER SUMMARY

While we can see from the literature that parents and caregivers play a central role in the support of interoceptive development, the processes by which these skills occur are still part of ongoing considerations and are likely a complex interplay between biology and environment – a classic example of the age-old nature–nurture debate and the need for a more interactional account of a phenomenon. While we have cited examples of the important role that social interactions play and the impacts that well-researched concepts such as attachment and the impacts of early childhood adversity may have on the development of accurate interoceptive abilities, we do not want to suggest that all responsibility falls with parents and caregivers. What we will see in the next chapter is that there are some people who find interoception difficult, such as autistic people, and also that there are strong influences to do with the ways that cultural groups operate which may impact on understandings of interoception and individual abilities.

CHAPTER 3

Interoceptive Atypicality

W E SAW IN THE LAST CHAPTER that the development of interoceptive abilities can be facilitated through co-regulation, and parents have been shown to play a key role in helping children develop awareness and correctly label internal bodily feelings. However, what we also know is that the development of interoceptive skills may remain a challenge for some people, and interoceptive challenges are frequently recognized in people who have particular labels such as autism spectrum disorder, anxiety, depression, schizophrenia, eating disorders, and alexithymia. Due to the involvement of interoception in so many psychological conditions, it has been proposed that it could be the underlying factor of many psychiatric disorders (Murphy *et al.*, 2017). Indeed, poor interoception is implicated in poor self-regulation, which, as Nigg (2017) reported, may also be implicated in many psychological and developmental disorders. What is common to the labels above is that they are characterized by difficulties with self-management and/or self-regulation. We have previously touched on the links in patterns of interoceptive abilities for those individuals displaying anxiety, and therefore this chapter will focus on neurodivergent individuals, specifically those who have a label of autism.

NEURODIVERSITY AND INTEROCEPTIVE SKILLS

Some individuals tend to show a variety of differences in interoceptive accuracy and awareness (Badoud & Tsakiris, 2017). This has been shown to be particularly important for autistic people who tend to be less sensitive to their own bodily signals (Mul *et al.*, 2018). In work by Fiene, Ireland, and Brownlow (2018), it was found that 75% of autistic participants in their sample reported some sort of interoceptive confusion. These differences appeared to be related to the display of autistic traits – as autistic traits increased, so too did interoceptive confusion. It is common to see reports of unusual sensory engagements for autistic people, and an area commonly reported in the literature is the unusual eating patterns of autistic children and adults. Parents commonly reflect on challenges of early feeding problems, food refusal, and failure to thrive for their autistic children. Therefore, it would seem that there are complex interactions between internal bodily states and health outcomes, which may be particularly relevant for the autistic population given their frequent interoceptive inaccuracy or lack of noticing altogether – Emma will provide some examples of this later on from her personal experience.

In their work, Fiene and colleagues observed that often autistic people develop highly sophisticated externally cued strategies through which to maintain their own body homeostasis and physiologically self-regulate. For example, some may rely on the time to act as a cue as to whether they are hungry or thirsty, or the weather forecast as to whether they should wear a jumper to keep warm. While these strategies may work to manage oneself to some degree, because they do not rely on internal bodily cues, they may unintentionally skew the information and consequent actions. For example, if the weather forecast is incorrect regarding temperature, we may get overheated, or may not realize that we need to drink more in very hot weather.

Fiene and colleagues propose that this reliance on external cues at the expense of accurate reading of internal cues may present risks to physical health and in more extreme cases could result in dehydration, heat exhaustion, or malnutrition.

In Emma's experience, inaccurate reading of internal cues has resulted in significant health risks, when a lack of ability to localize pain resulted in a delay in receiving emergency medical treatment. One of Emma's autistic friends had a stroke that was not responded to by doctors or paramedics because she did not notice the changes in her body.

Similarly, autistic people have been shown to have difficulties with sensory processing, and there are ample examples of sensory challenge and overwhelm in both research findings and experiential accounts. While much research has focused on the external stimuli to this, internal signals and accurate reading of these have also been identified as a factor (DuBois et al., 2016). This difficulty that autistic people seem to have in reading their own body's signals has far-reaching implications for behaviour. Think about the child in the busy classroom, surrounded by loud and unpredictable noise. If they don't notice that their body is trying to tell them that they are starting to feel anxious, with their heart starting to beat quickly and their body temperature increasing slightly, it may be too late for them to manage their own behaviour by the time the teacher shouts to issue instructions to the class. By then the child may have entered self-preservation mode, with the external behaviours demonstrating overwhelm. Consequently, these children are frequently perceived as being dysregulated or deliberately naughty, as opposed to needing support to identify and manage their emotions.

Emma recalls numerous occasions when she would become dysregulated, only to find out many years later that this occurred every time she became very hungry. Emma rarely notices when she is beginning to get hungry and so would not eat in time to prevent 'hangry'. Another personal example from Emma of dysregulation caused by inaccurate reading of internal sensory cues is related to temperature. Curious as to why she felt that she was hot when no one around was hot, Emma used her hands to 'feel' the temperature of her limbs. What she discovered was that when she assumed she was hot, her feet were actually often so cold that her toes were blueish in colour and very cold to the touch. Previously, Emma had experienced emotional distress when 'feeling hot' and would either put the air-conditioner on or remove outer layers of clothing, neither of which would ease her emotional distress. Realizing that the distress was due to cold feet allowed Emma to change strategies and put socks or slippers on. Either of these strategies reduced her distress effectively.

We briefly mentioned in Chapter 1 the links that have been proposed between anxiety and interoception. Autistic people have been shown to demonstrate high rates of anxiety. Furthermore, around 50% of autistic individuals also experience alexithymia, which is characterized by atypical emotional expression and recognition (Mul *et al.*, 2018; Murphy *et al.*, 2017). However, researchers have not yet reached a consensus on how poor interoception and alexithymia are linked, or if, indeed, they are one and the same (Fiene *et al.*, 2018). Paulus and Stein (2010) propose that if we accept that interoception is the basis for asking ourselves how we feel, and amplified interoceptive states become very 'noisy' for an individual, and consequently difficult to process and manage, it is easy to see how this can facilitate increased states of anxiety. For autistic people, managing these signals can be an ongoing challenge, both in terms of recognition and accurate labelling and consequent action. Additionally, if autistic individuals do not notice when they are starting to get anxious, they won't address their building anxiety, which will then continue to build. High levels of anxiety can then result, which may also leave the person anxious about experiencing anxiety and so drive an anxiety cycle.

HOW CAN WE MEASURE INTEROCEPTION?

What we hope is clear so far is that interoceptive skills and abilities are complex and often hard to define. Just thinking about our own interpretations of what it feels like for our bodies to be in states of anxiety, hunger, or thirst means the accurate interpretation of a whole range of signals, with these internal signals frequently needing further interpretation in relation to the external contexts in which we find ourselves. There is little wonder that children find this difficult!

The challenges in reporting our own internal states have also led to challenges for researchers and clinicians in the development of accurate tools to assess and measure interoceptive abilities. If we are going to provide supports to assist people in developing their own interoceptive awareness, it would make sense that we need to be able to identify when this might be challenging for people. Mahler (2016) has developed two tools based on her clinical practice work, the Interoceptive Awareness Interview and the Caregiver Questionnaire for Interoceptive Awareness. These tools enable the self-report of individuals and also the external reporting by parents and caregivers of a child's interoceptive abilities. Such tools provide useful frameworks for clinicians in the assessment of interoception in their clients.

Previous work by Emma developed a tracking tool to help support the identification of interoceptive skills in a school-based intervention in Australia (Goodall, 2021). The tracking sheet allowed schools to record the development of interoceptive skills and help to break down components of interoceptive signals for both students and teachers. This can be seen below.

Body awareness (interoception)	Date when achieved	Internal signals that tell me	How I can respond to this in a helpful way
I can feel my muscles tense and relax			
I can feel when I am cold			
I can feel when I am hot			
I know when I am thirsty			
I know when I am hungry			
I know when I need to go to the toilet			
I know when I am in pain			
I know where it hurts when I am in pain			
I know when I feel unwell			
I can explain what the problem is when I feel unwell			

I know when I am starting to get upset		
I know when I am starting to get anxious		
I know when I am starting to get frustrated		
I know when I am starting to get bored		
I know when I am starting to get angry		
I know when I am getting over-excited		
I know when I am getting overwhelmed		
I know when I am tired		
I know when I am happy		
I know when I am calm		

What this tool helps with is not only clarity concerning particular behaviours, but also the keeping of a record that can be referred back to in order to determine when developments in these areas occurred. Such records proved incredibly useful not only for teachers in their reporting and tracking of behaviours, but also for students in reflecting on their engagement with their bodily signals. The end column 'How I can respond to this in a helpful way' is important for students to know what to do in response to internal body signals. For example, if you develop an awareness of what your thirst sensations feel like, but do not know that drinking water is a helpful response, then you may well still not drink water when you are thirsty, much as you did not drink water when you did not recognize the thirst signals. It is not always obvious to students what a helpful response might be to a feeling or emotion, so having the option to record this normalizes the learning needed in this area.

When we are trying to evaluate our own or someone else's interoception, it is not enough to ask: 'Do you know when you feel hot?' Many people will say yes, whether or not they actually do know. Instead, you need to ask: 'How do you know when you feel hot?' or 'What signals does your body show you (or make) so that you know when you are getting hot?' Some examples of questions you might ask are:

1. Do you get overwhelmed ('lose it') easily and/or frequently?
2. Do you know that you are going to need to go to the toilet in a while or do you know when you really need to go now?
3. Can you tell when you are getting hot or cold and respond in ways that prevent you from getting hot or cold?

These questions can also be used as an observational tool for children and young people who may not yet understand these concepts.

Other tools have also been developed that aim to quantify interoceptive abilities through the use of scales. An example of a short questionnaire that has been developed based on a general population, including autistic people, is the Interoception Sensory Questionnaire – ISQ (Adults) developed by Charlotte and her colleagues (Fiene *et al.*, 2018). You can see the questions below – see where you sit in terms of how well you can connect with your own internal bodily feelings.

1 = not at all true of me; 7 = very true of me

		1	2	3	4	5	6	7
1	I have difficulty making sense of my body's signals unless they are very strong							
2	I tend to rely on visual reminders (e.g. times on the clock) to help me know when to eat and drink							
3	I have difficulty feeling my bodily need for food							
4	I'm not sure how my body feels when it's a hot day							
5	I find it difficult to describe feelings like hunger, thirst, hot, or cold							
6	Sometimes I don't know how to interpret sensations I feel within my body							
7	If I injure myself badly, even though I can feel it, I don't feel the need to do much about it							
8	I only notice I need to eat when I'm in pain or feeling nauseous or weak							

		1	2	3	4	5	6	7
9	There are times when I am only aware of changes in my body because of the reactions of other people							
10	I find it difficult to read the signs and signals within my own body (e.g. when I have hurt myself or I need to rest)							
11	I have difficulty understanding when I am hungry or thirsty							
12	I find it difficult to identify some of the signals that my body is telling me (e.g. if I'm about to faint or I've overexerted myself)							
13	It is difficult for me to describe what it feels like to be hungry, thirsty, hot, cold, or in pain							
14	I am confused about my bodily sensations							
15	I have difficulty locating injury in my body							
16	Sometimes, when my body signals a problem, I have difficulty working out what the problem might be							
17	I don't tend to notice feelings in my body until they're very intense							
18	I find it difficult to put my internal bodily sensations into words							
19	Even when I know that I am hungry, thirsty, in pain, hot, or cold, I don't feel the need to do anything about it							
20	Even when I know that I am physically uncomfortable, I do not act to change my situation							

Once you have answered all of the questions, you need to total your score. How did you do? As a guide, scores above 71 indicate some level of interoceptive confusion unless signals from the body are extreme. Scores above 94 indicate significant confusion with interoceptive states. As a general guide, Fiene and colleagues found that autistic adults typically had a mean score of 89, with their neurotypical peers scoring a mean of 48.

CHALLENGING DOMINANT WAYS OF THINKING

What we can see from above is that some people do find it difficult to connect with their body, resulting in the display of reduced interoceptive abilities. However, as well as individual differences, we also need to consider the possibility of broader cultural impacts on our understandings of body and self. One such example is that of trauma, and particularly intergenerational trauma, where patterns of interoceptive challenges are frequently evident.

Yehuda and colleagues (2016) showed in their research the significant impacts of intergenerational trauma. In the context of Aboriginal peoples, Canadian research has highlighted the complex contexts that contribute to the intergenerational transmission of trauma in Aboriginal/First Nations people (Aguiar & Halseth, 2015). In Australia, Nathan (2019, p.371) writes about the 'hurting hearts that are endemic in the post-colonial trauma' of Aboriginal Australians. Hurting hearts is a concept that may not resonate with behaviour coaches or teachers as a possible cause of difficulties with self-regulation, but it sits well with understandings of Māori (Te Whare Tapa Whā) and Pacific Island models of health and well-being which are more holistic than dominant culture models of health and/or well-being in Western nations. These models provide a framework for understanding the relationship between context and well-being, including emotional health. Emotional health is based on the ability to recognize and manage your emotions. As we can see in Figures 3.1 and 3.2, the understanding of this can be much more holistic in some cultures.

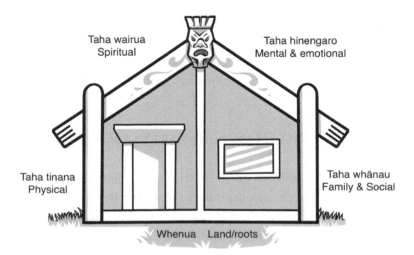

FIGURE 3.1: MĀORI HEALTH MODEL
Source: adapted from Durie (n.d.)

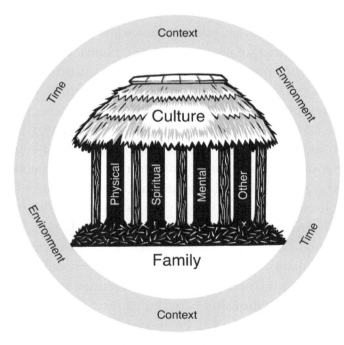

FIGURE 3.2: PASIFIKA HEALTH MODEL
Source: adapted from Pulotu-Endemann (2007)

The Māori model includes *wairua* (spirit or spiritual), the role of the *whānau* (family), and the balance of the *hinengaro* (mind), as well as the *tinana* (body or physical manifestations of illness). Pulotu-Endemann's (2007) Pasifika health model includes even more domains that show the cultural links between health and well-being in ways that more closely reflect Aboriginal Australian cultures. If well-being is understood as positive psychosocial functioning, then self-regulation is an antecedent to well-being (Balzarotti *et al.*, 2016), which in the above models fits into and impacts relationships/family, spiritual, physical, and mental health.

If we think about this a little bit more in terms of links to interoception, we can see that the implications for our understandings are quite significant. So far, we have considered interoception to be an individual experience that relies on an individual being accurately in touch with their own internal bodily feelings. As such, this is deemed the responsibility of us as individuals not only to master this understanding but to manage our own behaviours accordingly. We can see from the two examples provided above that there are alternative views on this – views that see the individual and their world as intertwined both in terms of their relationships with others and also the relationship of themselves with bigger entities such as their environment and the historical, collective, and cultural relationship with land and belonging. While interoception may therefore be partly physiological signals, the separation or integration of individuals with their broader context will have significant impact on their overall sense of well-being, with potential impact on their ability to read their own body. It further highlights the role of caregivers and others in the co-facilitation of interoceptive skills, meaning that managing and regulating our own behaviours may be everybody's business.

CHAPTER SUMMARY

In summary, what we can see is that the development and mastery of interoception can be complicated, with some people, such as autistic people, having more difficulty with this than others. However, what is important to remember is the key role that others may play in helping us with what could easily be considered something solely internal and individual to each of us. We know from Chapter 2 that parents and caregivers play a crucial role in the co-facilitation of the development of interoceptive abilities through their explicit identification and focus on the internal signals of children. We can also see that when we think differently about how we as an individual locate ourselves within our cultural contexts and focus on the intertwining nature of culture, time, environment, family, and individual, the responsibility for self-management becomes more shared. Key to this sharing is the roles that others may play in the development of interoceptive skills and the following chapters will explore some practical strategies in supporting this. Although individuals may embark on a solo journey to improve their interoception, the activities in the following chapters can also be used by families as well as professionals working with children, young people, and adults.

CHAPTER 4

Tuning in to Your 'Self' – Developing and Improving Interoception

W E CAN SEE FROM THE PREVIOUS CHAPTERS that tuning into the feelings and signals from ourselves is central for the successful management of feelings and emotions and self-regulating these. But how do we know how we feel about a thing, an event, or an experience? Our brain collects and interprets a range of input about the thing (external signals) and how our body has reacted to it (internal signals) and compares these signals with past signals. So, for example, if you see a large red shape in the distance, your brain will reflect on previous large red shapes and what they meant or turned out to be. Even though this all sounds very automatic, there are some aspects of feeling that are not automatic. Noticing is key. An example of this is when you are eating rice and all of a sudden realize that there is a texture in the food that shouldn't have been there. If you were paying full attention, you would have noticed the stone in the rice before putting it in your mouth. Through noticing, you could have prevented the uncomfortable moment you bit on the stone in the rice. This sort of thing may be mildly annoying for some individuals but completely overwhelming for others, particularly those on the autism spectrum. Emma recalls that she really struggles to eat any more of the food on her plate if there has been an unexpected texture such as a stone in the rice or sand in mussels.

Another example that we gave previously can be observed when children fall over when they are playing. Children often get up and keep playing, especially if they are not seriously injured. However, if an adult comes over to check they are OK, then the tears may start. Not necessarily because they are in pain; instead, it seems to be a learnt 'expected behaviour'. In contrast, children and even adults who do not 'notice their pain' may have blood running down their leg for a few minutes before they notice it, and are then genuinely surprised, wondering what happened to cause the injury. We are all different in how we react to these things. Emma reflects that she is a curious mix of both of these. With heightened sensitivity to most sharp pain, she can scream or cry at the tiniest cut, because it is noticeable. On the other hand, she can get changed for bed and then notice massive bruises and have no idea how they were acquired.

Interoception is that conscious perception or noticing of internal body signals. When we aren't tuned in to our internal body signals, even though our body is experiencing and signalling feelings or emotions, we may not notice the signal and so not 'feel the experience'. An example of this is when you are really focused on something that you enjoy, and suddenly you realize you need to go to the toilet – right now. You have missed all the early signals that you are going to need to go to the toilet, because you were totally focused on what you were doing. It was only when it became urgent and you finally noticed the body signals that you realized that you needed to go to the toilet. This example may be taken to the extreme for individuals with poor intero-ceptive awareness of their bladders. They may not notice until they urgently need to go to the toilet, regardless of what they are doing. This is often apparent in schools, where students may run out of class urgently needing to go to the toilet. Teachers may respond with punishment, assuming that the student 'could have gone at the previous break, or waited until the next', whereas, in fact, the student didn't know that they were going to need to go soon, and they are not able to hold on any longer.

In earlier chapters, we spoke about the development of interoceptive abilities. For babies, the developing awareness of feelings is the beginning of the experience and expression of more complicated feelings and emotions, all of which sit on the foundational skill of noticing and being connected to your internal self – that is, your skills of interoception. Often the first part of themselves that babies notice and obviously connect with are their hands. We can tell when a baby is aware of their hands because they start to wave them around, stare at them, and put them in their mouths. Interestingly, it takes some time for babies to differentiate between their hands and other people's hands. The next body part that babies seem to enjoy consciously exploring is their feet. Many a parent has marvelled at the way their baby is exploring their toes with their mouth. It is important at this stage of development that young children get a range of experiences to help them develop good awareness of the biofeedback from their hands and feet in different situations. As you watch a young child learning to pick up and move things with their hands, they are starting to learn exactly how hard to grip different things.

There are three main reasons why children and young people and even adults can struggle with managing their feelings and emotions:

1. Disempowerment, disenfranchisement, and/or trauma – these can be both personally experienced and inter-generational (Shields, Cicchetti, & Ryan, 1994).
2. Mental health difficulties such as anxiety and depression (Zamariola *et al.*, 2019).

3. Developmental difficulties that have self-management and self-regulation challenges (Gross & Thompson, 2007).

It has been reported that between 25% and 50% (a quarter to a half) of children and young people will experience a mental health difficulty (Zamariola *et al.*, 2019). Rates are higher for individuals with disability than those without. It is not inevitable that your child will develop a mental health difficulty, even if they have multiple disabilities. However, without a good understanding of their emotions and feelings, it may be more likely.

The best protective factors for mental health are feeling valued, having a sense of belonging, and having at least one person care about you (Michalski *et al.*, 2020). This means that you as a parent or educator can be that one person who cares, and this can be invaluable. Another reason that children and young people can struggle with their emotions and feelings is biological. When anyone experiences a significant amount of stress or trauma, human biology creates a number of feedback loops that can increase the likelihood of behaviours that can appear challenging, naughty, or bad. As researchers Evans and Kim (2013) suggest, numerous stressors that add up for an individual can disrupt children's self-regulation processes that work to support children in managing difficult situations.

Chronic stress also impacts the ability of children and young people to learn as it reduces the integration of new information into existing memories (Vogel & Schwabe, 2016). For this reason, if a child is not able to learn new skills or knowledge, it is important to consider their levels of stress. Stress or distress impacts humans in a number of ways. A small amount of stress is important as it helps humans to learn, but too much is not good for us at all. Too much stress or trauma can lead to us not being able to tell the difference between life-threatening events and other events, meaning that we go into survival mode when we don't need to. Using the strategies in this book will be useful to help decrease the biological impact of stress in the moment and over time. Chapter 5 outlines several practical strategies that you can use to help children and young people to manage their feelings and understand internal body signals.

Recognizing our own internal bodily signals is crucial in managing the impacts of stress and allowing less chronic impacts of the external world on our internal being. The link between interoceptive awareness and interoceptive accuracy is complex, however. Without awareness, you cannot have accuracy, but even with interoceptive awareness, you may not have interoceptive accuracy. So, for example, you may have excellent interoceptive awareness for pain but very poor interoceptive accuracy for pain. What this means is that you might interpret a paper cut as being as painful as a major injury. Similarly, you may also be unable to accurately locate where pain is coming from unless there is an external visual cue such as a cut.

There are other words for interoceptive awareness that have been used more commonly, such as biofeedback, somatic awareness, mindful body awareness, and connection to self. Whatever words are used, it is clear that many children and adults do not have optimal interoceptive awareness and therefore do not have good interoceptive accuracy, as we have discussed in previous chapters. This is important because without good interoception, people cannot self-regulate and self-manage as easily, or in some cases at all. This difficulty with self-regulation and self-management seems to arise when people don't notice emerging emotions and so cannot do anything about them, which leads to those emotions intensifying, or, as described in Dan Siegel's hand model of the brain, 'big emotions'. It is harder to control your behaviour when you are enraged than it is when you are mildly annoyed!

In addition, noticing, though vital, is not enough in and

of itself. Let's take stomachache to understand what else is required in order to be able to self-manage or self-regulate. Stomachache is an internal body signal that could be signalling a myriad of things. We can get stomachache in any or all of the following instances: food poisoning, period pain, constipation, extreme hunger, illness, overeating, falling in love, or pulled stomach muscles during exercise. How does an individual tell whether they pulled their muscles or are falling in love? There may be other contextual clues that hint at which it might be, but sometimes these can be fuzzy. For example, if they have just exercised with someone they might be attracted to, how can they then tell the difference? This is where it is important to notice not just one internal body signal but a collection of them. Feelings and emotions, such as love, hunger, satiation, and sadness, are signalled not by just one internal body signal but several. The trick for the individual is to attend to each of these and make sense of the signals that they are receiving.

Without making sense of these signals, it is hard to self-manage or self-regulate. Taking the example of the individual with stomachache who exercised with someone that they might be attracted to, if they decide that they were in love, they might end up with a very sore stomach because they were responding to an inaccurate feeling, rather than the actual feeling of pulled muscles during exercise, resulting in pulling them again soon after.

Think about yourself, when you are tired – how does your body feel? Some people may notice that they feel tired when their eyes feel heavy, their body feels sluggish overall, and they are yawning. Other people may have all these same signals or other signals and not notice them at all. If you feel tired, you are more likely to rest or go to bed, whereas if you don't notice that you are tired, you may keep working or engaging in activities that can result in accidents if done when too tired.

ACHIEVING BALANCE

Against the background of the survival instinct of the human species, including our biological need for and drive towards homeostasis, interoceptive awareness can be broadly split into three categories, which, when combined, enable people to understand themselves, self-regulate, and self-manage.

Bodies seek to be in a dynamic state of equilibrium, known in biology as homeostasis. Homeostasis has many elements, including body temperature, fluid balance, and physical well-being. Feelings arise in changes of body state when we are no longer in homeostasis. For example, our body overheats and so we feel the sensation of hot and the desire or need to cool ourselves down. Humans also seek equilibrium in social interactions and interactions with the wider world. Our survival instinct is triggered by sensations of fear or assumptions of threats to our 'selves'. Our feelings are at the heart of the way we interact with others and the way we are. However, if we do not have a good sense of self, we are not noticing our body signals, and so in effect do not 'feel' our feelings. Figure 4.1 shows the role that interoceptive skills play in achieving homeostasis.

Self-regulation is commonly understood in education settings to be self-control, whereby an individual moderates or controls their emotions and behaviour in order to follow the social norms of the context in which they are in. This is sometimes referred to as self-control. Self-management, on the other hand, is related to the control of or actioning of behaviours in order to fulfil biological needs, such as hunger or being too hot or cold – for example, drinking water when thirsty or putting a sweater on when cold. Self-management is more obviously linked to homeostasis, as evidenced by the need for our bodies to be within a particular temperature range, have energy input through food and output through waste elimination, and control energy usage by muscle movement, etc.

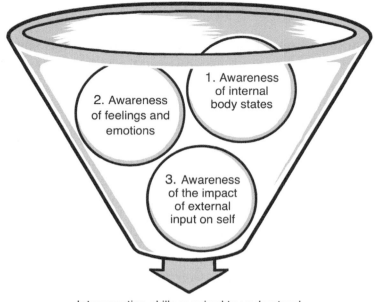

Interoception skills required to understand
self, self-regulate and self-manage

FIGURE 4.1: BIOLOGICAL NEED FOR HOMEOSTASIS
AND HUMAN SURVIVAL INSTINCT

THE IMPORTANCE OF CO-REGULATION

When children and young people have not yet developed
interoception skills, they will struggle not only with their own
emotions but with social interactions – even just being around
others may be difficult for them to manage. As we have seen
earlier, little children are still developing their awareness and
understanding of their internal body signals, so it is difficult for
them to self-manage their needs and feelings, and to self-regulate their wants and emotions. Instead, they need co-regulating
by others. Co-regulating is when other people help someone
to manage their needs and feelings, wants and emotions, in
helpful ways – for example, by encouraging a tired toddler to

sleep, feeding a hungry baby, and reminding a hot teenager to take their sweatshirt off to cool down and have a drink of water to rehydrate.

Anyone can benefit from co-regulation, but individuals who struggle to notice and accurately recognize their internal body signals *need* this co-regulation. If we think about a person who doesn't notice or recognize when they are cold, we can identify a number of issues that may occur:

1. The person may get very cold leading to hypothermia or frostbite.
2. They may become unwell from being too cold too often.
3. They may get grumpy or anxious.
4. They may finally realize they are cold only when they can see a blueish tinge to their feet or other body parts.

In previous chapters, Emma reflected on the challenges of thermoregulating. She found the benefits of co-regulation of this from others in that others were able to notice whether she was getting hot or cold before she could, using external cues. Friends, family, or even colleagues would let Emma know when she was getting hot or cold and suggest helpful ways to manage this. Emma found that following their advice meant she was more able to manage her feelings and emotions consistently and so behave in professional and appropriate ways at all times.

Personally, I struggle to thermoregulate – that is, to manage my body temperature. I cannot tell that I am getting hot or cold until I am very overheated or very cold. Interestingly, I can often assume I am very hot, but when I use my hand to check how hot or cold my skin is, my feet and ankles will be significantly colder than the rest of my body. I get angry very quickly when I am hot, but only realized this after lots of input from close friends and family. However, I also get angry more easily when I am hungry and can't always tell the difference without either taking my temperature or doing a quick checklist on context, such as: when did I last eat, what did I eat, what is the temperature of the room/place I am in, am I wearing clothes suitable for that kind of temperature? In this way, I can make an educated guess.

Often, people who know a person very well can often tell them they need to eat before the person knows themselves that they are hungry. They are co-regulating, which as long as it is done in a kind and caring way, rather than being controlling or patronizing, is very helpful and often much appreciated.

As we have already seen in Chapters 2 and 3, interoceptive abilities can be divergent. Research and anecdotal evidence – for example, from within the autistic community – indicate that even early interoceptive awareness is atypical in autistics. This may be why some autistics learn to walk on their tiptoes or the side of their feet. The biofeedback is much greater when walking with your feet in these positions than in the traditional position. Give it a go and see for yourself!

Children with a range of other neurodevelopmental differences, including those who have intergenerational trauma or first-hand experiences of trauma, also tend to present with atypical interoception, often experiencing significantly lower awareness of internal body signals than other children. Children who have very limited or no personal interactions with adults also struggle to develop their interoception. For this reason, it is important that parents and other caregivers interact with children to help develop the child's awareness of self. It is never too late to improve your interoceptive awareness and accuracy through simple mindful body awareness activities. Examples of practical strategies to manage emotions can be found in Chapter 5, which includes a range of interoceptive activities.

Atypical and, in particular, poor interoception can have huge impacts both in the short and long term. In terms of lifelong impact, take the issue of going to the toilet. Before going home at the end of a workday, many adults will take into account the time of day, traffic conditions, and expected commute time to decide whether or not to go to the toilet before they leave. However, other adults do not have such good interoceptive awareness of their bladder or bowel and don't know when they need to use the toilet until they really *need* to go. These adults may have to stop on their way home to use a public toilet, and in some cases may avoid leaving the house due to their fear of not being able to get to a toilet in time.

When we are being toilet-trained, we normally learn that we are going to need to go soon from the adults around us. They tell us that we are wiggling or clutching and we need to go to the toilet. Over time, children start to be more aware of how their body feels when their bladder is full or their bowel needs emptying. They start to be able to anticipate it and know how long they can wait. Children and adults with poor bladder/bowel interoceptive awareness and/or nerve damage are not able to wait, but *need* to go when they notice that they need to go.

Some inaccurate readings of signals can lead to significant health impacts for people. For example, a lack of awareness of thirst or hunger can also have a range of impacts, dehydration and failure to thrive being a couple of them. For you as co-regulators, it can sometimes be hard to teach or learn the internal body signals for thirst and hunger, but it is easy to use visuals to support an awareness of our body. If hydration charts and Bristol stool charts are put on the back of the toilet door or on the wall next to the toilet, they are clear visual supports. We have included these charts in Chapter 5 for your reference.

Remember that noticing and then accurately labelling feelings and signals can be a challenge for some. There may be signals that we think should be obvious such as dehydration causing headaches, grumpiness, difficulty in concentrating and learning, and sore throats, contributing to constipation, and in the longer term leading to possible kidney damage. However, many neurodivergent people have atypical interoceptive awareness of pain and may not notice the pain of constipation. On the other hand, it is possible to have severe medical complications from drinking too much water, which is more likely to happen when someone is unable to notice if they are thirsty or not. Research by Fiene (2018) indicated that autistic adults with atypical interoceptive awareness of thirst either drank far too much water or nowhere near enough.

WHAT DOES THIS MEAN FOR OUR FEELINGS AND EMOTIONS?

Feelings and emotions are collections of body signals that are processed in our brain and interpreted as particular concepts such as hunger, thirst, sleepy, happy, and angry. Feelings are hints to help us self-manage our selves. If we go back to thinking about a baby, a baby does not know if someone crying is experiencing a pleasant, unpleasant, or neutral emotion. Babies can react to crying by ignoring it or responding with tears of their own or even giggling. An adult seeing someone cry will usually look at the context to decide how to react. If the person is injured and crying, there will be an assumption that the person is experiencing an unpleasant emotion, requiring care, kindness, and sympathy. However, someone crying and laughing may be assumed to be experiencing a pleasant emotion, with no response required. A child who has been taught that crying is what sad people do may not be able to distinguish between happy and sad tears. A child who does not know what it feels like to be sad will not understand what an unpleasant experience that can be. This child may appear to have no empathy, but it may be more a lack of their own interoceptive awareness. If someone has a lack of connection to their own feelings, it is hard for them to connect to the feelings of others.

Psychologists used to think that everyone experiences emotions in the same way. For example, anger would be mainly felt in the top half of the body and in the arms, whereas envy is mostly contained to sensations in the head. A series of body maps have been released which mapped where, on average, the perception of various emotions was experienced (Nummenmaa *et al.*, 2014). Damasio and Carvalho (2013) suggested that these body maps provide convincing evidence to support the role of interoception in emotion – that the experience of emotion is largely based on interoception. They defined feelings as mental constructs of the conscious perception of internal body states. It is important to note that these emotion body maps are based on the averaging of where individuals report the body sensations for particular emotions. This would mean that if half the people felt the emotion at the top of their head and half in their toes, on the averaged body map the sensation would appear to be felt in the centre of the body.

However, we know that people do experience things slightly differently. If you have experienced prolonged stress, you may feel it in your neck, whereas other people can feel stress as tension in their shoulders or lower back. This illustrates that different people do feel emotions in different places. Parents often notice subtle body changes in their children that signal changing feelings and emotions. For example, a child who is getting tired may move more slowly and a child who is getting frustrated may tense their hands.

Furthermore, the expression of feelings and emotions is both culturally and individually based. For example, it is important in some cultures to be as outwardly expressive as possible with whole-body language and tone/cadence and volume of voice. In other cultures, keeping as passive/neutral a body and face as possible is the norm. For example, Emma currently has neighbours of Italian descent who use their hands and faces to emphasize feelings and emotions, and other neighbours from China who have much more neutral body language styles.

The difference between understanding our feelings and emotions and basic interoceptive awareness is that emotions and most feelings are represented by a collection of body state changes, whereas basic interoceptive awareness is of a single body state change. Take, for example, interoceptive awareness of a spasm in your abdomen area. This could be linked to a number of different feelings or emotions – feeling sick, hungry, afraid, period pain, upset tummy, love, excitement, etc. Only when a second and/or third body sensation is noticed and put together with or without additional contextual cues can the person connect to their emotion.

This is why some people, particularly children, may say that they are bored when they actually mean a variety of different emotions. They recognize that their body feels different in some way to when they are fine, but they are not sure how. They may have been told they were bored when they were noticing a difference, and so associate the word 'bored' with any internal feeling of different. When people are still developing their interoception, it is important not to tell them how they are feeling. Instead, describing their body signals and offering some suggestions about what these signals might mean is more useful.

For example, if a young person appears to have tight shoulders and arms, with hands spread wide and held tense, describing these will help the young person connect to their own body's signals so that over time they can feel these signals independently. You might add that you 'wonder if these signals are for frustration or anger or anxiety' and then explore contextual cues that might help explain what the young person is feeling.

If we go back to the example of spasm in the abdomen, describing other small body signals, such as clutching at their tummy or putting their hand up to their mouth, will help to discriminate between possible emotions and narrow it down further. Many teenage girls struggle to manage their periods because they do not notice the body signals that announce menstruation. It can help to be more explicit about body signals in puberty education rather than just focusing on what happens with periods.

Our feelings and emotions have both contextual and biological drivers. For example, hunger can be driven purely by the body when it is needing nutrients and driven by contextual prompts such as seeing or smelling food. Pain can be physical, which is usually a biological process, or emotional, which is often based on a situation or other contextual cues, such as a loved one moving away or dying.

Stress is both the perception of a threat or pressure on the self and the physiological response of the body to threats/ pressure. It can result in both feelings and emotions. The perception of a serious threat, whether real or imagined, can set off a hormonal cascade that leads to our survival instinct taking over. However, lower-level threats can be experienced as feeling stressed, and this feeling of stress is still associated with the sympathetic nervous system (SNS) and increased cortisol levels.

Early humans relied on their SNS to keep them safe from danger: when our SNS goes into overload, our survival instinct takes over. Figure 4.2 shows how this balancing act may appear.

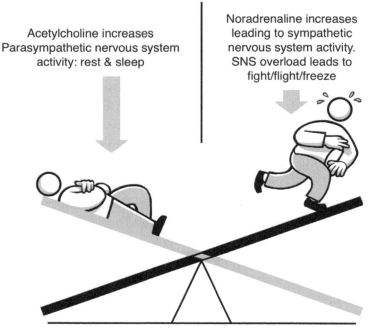

Acetylcholine increases Parasympathetic nervous system activity: rest & sleep

Noradrenaline increases leading to sympathetic nervous system activity. SNS overload leads to fight/flight/freeze

FIGURE 4.2: BALANCING THE SYMPATHETIC NERVOUS SYSTEM
Source: Goodall, 2019

Nowadays, our survival instinct is regularly being used to respond to perceived threats more than actual danger to our lives. This is because many of us are not well connected to our bodies, feelings, and emotions. We do not know when we are beginning to be stressed (or angry or tired) and so do not do anything about it. Not doing something about a feeling means that the feeling continues to grow and grow. A bit of stress becomes a huge amount of stress, anger can turn into rage, and tiredness can become exhaustion. Our bodies like to be in balance, in homeostasis, and being so out of balance distresses our bodies. In order to get back into homeostasis, we need to do something. That something is the basis of self-managing.

When individuals experience chronic stress, which can be for many reasons, such as poverty, lack of access to safety or food, bullying, and long-term pain or illness, this chronic stress can impact both physical and mental health. It appears that long-term chronic stress can also decrease interoceptive awareness, possibly as part of our survival mechanisms, in the same way that interoceptive awareness can be negatively impacted by trauma, as we discussed earlier. After all, it is better for our mental health to not actively feel significant trauma.

REGAINING BALANCE

When we are out of balance, to get back into homeostasis we need to do something helpful to return our body to balance. If we are overheated, we need to do things to cool down, such as drink water or turn the air conditioning on. Knowing what to do relies on both understanding our options but, more importantly, reading the interoceptive signals first. If you do not know you are dehydrated, because you do not notice your body signals that you are thirsty, then you will not drink any water. This is where the hydration chart visuals can be useful. You do not need to notice or recognize a dry throat; you simply need to notice that your urine is dark and smelly, and that this means you should drink. Chapter 5 discusses strategies for managing this in more detail.

Our survival instinct drives our actions and overrides our emotions and feelings. It is the ultimate in self-managing. For example, if a large snake slithers out of the grass and into our path, we do not want to think, 'Oh, a snake', then notice our heart rate race, then feel panic, and then react. Instead, to ensure our survival, we want our survival instinct to take over. As is seen in Figure 4.3, this may be a circular process.

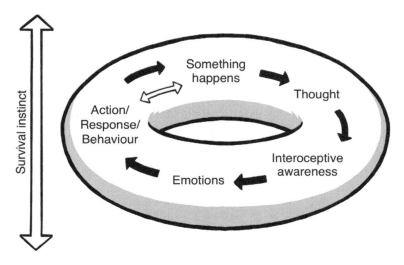

FIGURE 4.3: MANAGING OUR SURVIVAL INSTINCT
Source: Goodall, 2019

In non-life-threatening situations, we do need to be able to notice our internal body signals and our feelings and emotions, so that we respond or behave appropriately. In the initial example regarding thirst, we can either use external signals and supports or internal signals. One is not inherently superior to the other; however, external signals are not available for everything, so it is useful to continually improve our interoceptive awareness.

Part of the difficulty for children and adults with atypical interoception is that we can become overly reliant on our survival instinct as we 'interpret' situations and events as life-threatening when they are not. This can also occur when people, including children, are chronically stressed. It is widely accepted that chronic stress has negative impacts on both physical and mental health. Research in the fields of psychology, psychiatry, and occupational therapy has shown that developing interoception improves mental health and well-being and the ability to self-manage and self-regulate.

When we are children, we expect and accept that people around us will take care of our needs and respond to our cries appropriately. However, as we get older, we do not expect other people to take care of our needs and we begin to self-manage. So, when we are hot, we will take our own jumper off, or, when thirsty, we will go and get a drink. Some children move straight into this rather than asking for or otherwise indicating needs, whereas others may not move from one to the other for months, maybe years. Both asking for others to meet our needs and doing things to meet our own needs rely on knowing what those needs are. This is why interoception is a prerequisite for self-managing.

As discussed earlier, with interactions that serve to co-regulate and clearly label body signals, feelings and emotions, and helpful responses, most children will continually improve their interoception over time. As interoception improves, and children learn the most effective helpful responses to their internal body signals, they are more and more able to self-regulate and self-manage. For individuals who do not continually improve their interoception due to neurodevelopmental differences, or those who lose some/all of their interoceptive awareness due to trauma, interoception can be improved over time through mindful body awareness activities. Helpful responses to internal body signals may need explicitly teaching to these individuals.

The interoception centre of the brain is the insula. We know from neuroscience research that in order to improve connections in our brain, to improve the functioning of any part of our brain, we need to use the connections repeatedly to hardwire or fix the new connections. In other words, the activities in this book will develop or improve your interoception, but in order to ensure that your brain is able to keep that improvement in interoceptive skills, the activities, or similar ones, need to be done two or three times a day for two to three months. Each time an activity is done, you are 'tuning in' to your internal body signals. This can be practised for anywhere between 30 seconds and 20 minutes at a time – whatever feels comfortable and can be fitted into your day easily.

CHAPTER SUMMARY

Interoception has been shown to be a key driver in individuals tuning in to their own body and accurately reading signals which enable the self-management of behaviour, feelings, and emotions. We can help ourselves and others to fine-tune our internal readings through various exercises, which can be as straightforward as visual aids to tap into external cues and map these on to internal cues, or more complex as we will discuss in the next chapters. Because trauma of any kind can 'turn down' our ability to feel our feelings and emotions, it is important that these activities are carried out in a safe space, when you are feeling OK. They are of no use during panic! This is because the survival brain is in control and there is no thinking going on, so any demand or request to do anything is likely to be interpreted as further danger by the reptile brain. If you are using these in a school, preschool, or residential setting, it is best to incorporate them into your day two or three times each day, so that they act as an emotional reset at typically difficult times of the day such as first thing in the morning, after breaks/recess, and after lunch. Parents may want to do the activities first thing in the morning, after school pick-up, and before bed.

People who experience significant trauma will lose some of their interoceptive skills and will require more practice during times they are feeling safe, to restore their interoception. It is important to find a space that feels safe so that people can get in tune with their bodies – this may take a little time and practice! However, it is worth the effort as we know that interoceptive awareness is considered a prerequisite for recognizing and managing our emotions.

The strategies and activities in the next chapter can be used with children and adults of any age. Where individuals have significant additional physical disabilities, it will be useful to seek out an occupational therapist to individualize the activities or design ones for the individual. Good interoceptive awareness and accuracy are a journey, the results of which can be seen in elite athletes who are aware of exactly where to place their hands or feet, exactly how much to move them, and with what force to execute particular moves.

CHAPTER 5

Practical Strategies to Manage Feelings

As WE HAVE EXPLAINED in previous chapters, feelings are collections of internal body signals that we interpret in particular ways. Our eyes and arms might feel heavy, our head be falling forward slightly, and our brain be feeling less clear. If we can notice all of these internal body signals and recognize them, we may work out that we are tired. However, if we are hyper-focused on what we are doing, then we are less likely to notice them. Noticing and even focusing on internal body signals can be thought of as mindful body awareness.

As explained in Chapter 4, for our brains to take on and be able to automatically use learnt skills, such as interoceptive awareness, we need to practise the skill often enough to create new 'hardwired connections' in our brains. For some people, a 20-minute session once a day is more effective, but for others three shorter 1–5-minute sessions of mindful body awareness activities are most useful. Either way, the activities need to be done for at least two to three months before the skills become embedded in the brain.

Whether you choose to do short or longer sessions yourself or with individuals that you teach or care for, the structure of an interoceptive/mindful body awareness activity is always the same. The following pages can be photocopied or pulled out to use. Essentially, these activities seek to use guided and conscious noticing of internal body signals.

ACTIVITY: MINDFUL AWARENESS OF OUR BODIES

Interoception activities always focus on just one change in body state as this enables the active noticing of internal body signals. Starting at rest, a change of body state is carried out by focusing attention on just one element of our body at once. The activities can focus on:

- muscles
- breathing
- temperature
- pulse.

Start by adopting an interoception activity or mindful body awareness pose shown in Figure 5.1. This is called the resting state.

Where can you feel things? It can be a little hard to tell in this resting state. Now do the same interoception activity or mindful body awareness pose again and this time focus on just one part of your body where you felt something the first time. Did you feel it more the second time?

Once this change in state has occurred and you are more in tune with your body and the signals it is telling you, the idea is to reflect or question 'Where can I feel that change in state?' while going back to the resting state. If you are doing the activity alone, then you would repeat the change in state while focusing on one of the places that you had already noticed or felt that particular change in state. This repeat of the change in body state with a conscious focus on a particular body part is interoceptive awareness or mindful body awareness.

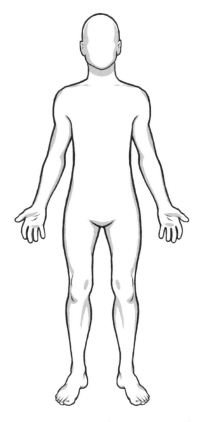

FIGURE 5.1: MINDFUL BODY AWARENESS POSE

If you are doing the activity with one or more others, then the activities must be done together and done twice, with the following steps each time:

1. All do the activity which changes *one* aspect of the body.
2. Talk about or sign or point to where you each felt something different in your body from before and during the activity.

3. Decide and agree on where you are going to focus on trying to feel something when you redo the activity. All redo the activity focusing on the body area/part that you decided on.

It is important to understand that everyone is different and that anyone can have some areas of good interoception and some of poor interoception. Doing these activities strengthens the ability of the brain to notice and interpret the body signals that make up feelings and emotions, and to be calm enough to self-regulate and helpfully express emotions and self-manage feelings and express needs and wants.

Some activities for each major part of the body follow, as well as a selection of breathing, temperature, and pulse activities. If you would like to watch and join in with some interoception videos, have a look at the interoception activities section of Emma's Healthy Possibilities YouTube Channel: www.youtube.com/channel/UCyIovxevV3W2l2WXHDBkKxA

Interoception activities playlist: www.youtube.com/watch?v=MJEmgG4wxJk&list=PLXTC2Uqaw5-3sO7rricA5pR2VChvT810H

FINGER STRETCH ACTIVITY

1. Starting at rest with relaxed hands, now change your body state by stretching your fingers as wide as possible.

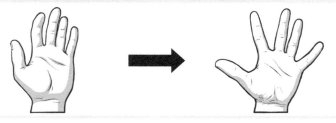

2. Go back to resting state. Where could you feel something different in your body between your relaxed hand and the stretched hand?

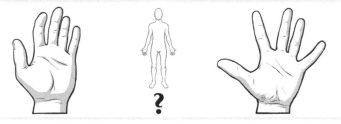

3. Now repeat the change in body state by doing the following AND mindfully focusing on one of the body parts identified in step 2.

Hint: You may feel something in the webbing between your fingers, on the palm, on the top of the palm, on your knuckles, down the sides of the fingers and/or thumb, across the back of the hand, in your wrist, and/or down the sides of your hand.

TOE CURL ACTIVITY

1. Starting at rest, with relaxed feet, now change your body state by curling your toes under as much as possible.

2. Go back to relaxing your toes. Where could you feel something different in your body between your relaxed toes and your curled-under toes?

3. Now repeat the change in body state by doing the following AND mindfully focusing on one of the body parts identified in step 2.

Hint: You may feel something in the toes, under the toes, on top of the toes, across the top of your foot, on the ball of your foot, in the arch of your foot, and/or along the side of your foot.

TOE/FOOT WALKING ACTIVITY

1. Starting at rest, walking on the spot with your feet flat on the floor, now change your body state by walking on your toes.

2. Go back to resting state. Where could you feel something different in your body between walking with feet flat and toe walking?

3. Now repeat the change in body state by doing the following AND mindfully focusing on one of the body parts identified in step 2.

Hint: You may feel something in the balls of your feet, your toes, and the top of your foot and ankle.

FINGER PULL ACTIVITY

1. Starting at rest with your fingers from one hand gently resting on the other, now change your body state by pressing the fingers tightly together at the same time as pulling your arms apart.

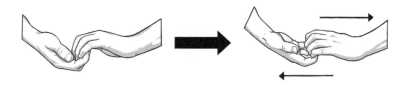

2. Go back to resting state. Where could you feel something different in your body between your resting state and the change?

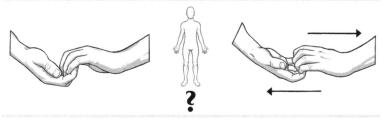

3. Now repeat the change in body state by doing the following AND mindfully focusing on one of the body parts identified in step 2.

Hint: You may feel something in the ends of your fingers, wrists, and/or shoulders.

LEG SQUATS ACTIVITY

1. Starting at rest, now change your body state by bending down into a squat position.

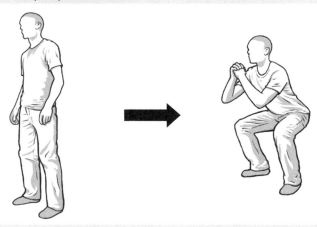

2. Go back to resting state. Where could you feel something different in your body between your resting state and the change?

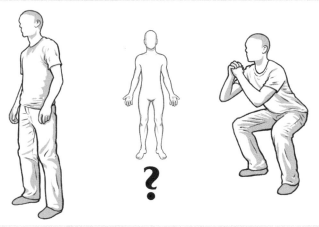

3. Now repeat the change in body state by doing the following AND mindfully focusing on one of the body parts identified in step 2.

Hint: You might feel something in your thighs, ankles, and glutes. This works the big muscles.

SHOULDER RISE/DROP ACTIVITY

1. Starting at rest, now change your body state by raising then lowering your shoulders in an exaggerated shoulder shrug.

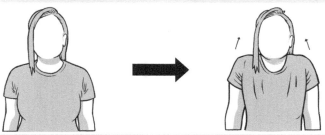

2. Go back to resting state. Where could you feel something different in your body between your resting state and the change?

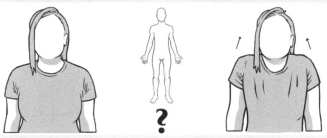

3. Now repeat the change in body state by doing the following AND mindfully focusing on one of the body parts identified in step 2.

Hint: You might feel something in the tops of your shoulders, your neck, and possibly your back.

ARM PULLS ACTIVITY

1. Starting at rest, now change your body state by bending one arm back and stretching this over your back.

2. Go back to resting state. Where could you feel something different in your body between your resting state and the change?

3. Now repeat the change in body state by doing the following AND mindfully focusing on one of the body parts identified in step 2.

Hint: You might feel something in your shoulders, the tops of your arms, and your back.

ARM STRETCHES ACTIVITY

1. Starting at rest, now change your body state by stretching your arms straight up in the air.

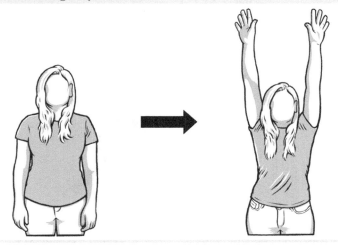

2. Go back to resting state. Where could you feel something different in your body between your resting state and the change?

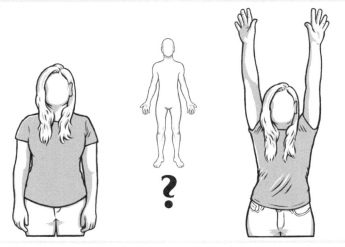

3. Now repeat the change in body state by doing the following AND mindfully focusing on one of the body parts identified in step 2.

Hint: You might feel something in your shoulder, neck, and back.

BELLY BREATHING ACTIVITY

1. Starting at rest, now change your body state by breathing in and filling your stomach with air.

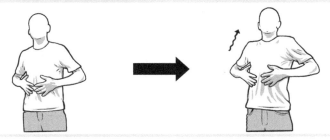

2. Go back to resting state. Where could you feel something different in your body between your resting state and the change?

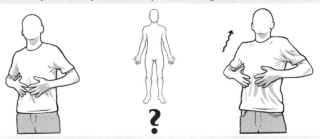

3. Now repeat the change in body state by doing the following AND mindfully focusing on one of the body parts identified in step 2.

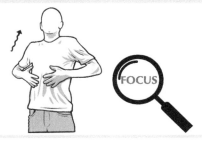

Hint: You may feel something in your belly but will also be aware of your breathing.

SIDE TWIST ACTIVITY

1. Starting at rest, now change your body state by twisting around to one side slowly, then the other.

2. Go back to resting state. Where could you feel something different in your body between your resting state and the change?

3. Now repeat the change in body state by doing the following AND mindfully focusing on one of the body parts identified in step 2.

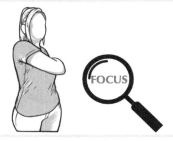

Hint: You may feel something down the sides of your body, your back, and possibly your neck.

LEG STRETCH ACTIVITY

1. Starting at rest, now change your body state by stretching your leg behind you and holding it with your hand.

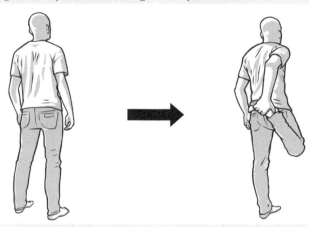

2. Go back to resting state. Where could you feel something different in your body between your resting state and the change?

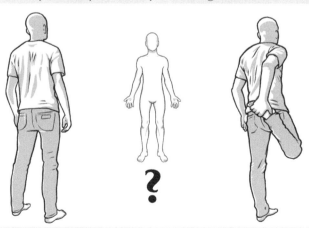

3. Now repeat the change in body state by doing the following AND mindfully focusing on one of the body parts identified in step 2.

Hint: You may feel something down your thigh and maybe in your ankle and the hand that is holding this.

The activities above are designed to teach individuals to become engaged with their body and both recognize and accurately interpret signals. However, there are two key areas of interoceptive awareness that are difficult to teach through these kinds of mindful body awareness, but easy to support using visual prompts. These are the areas of thirst/hydration and constipation, which were both discussed in Chapter 4. These can be supported using the visual prompts of a hydration chart and a Bristol stool chart respectively. These can be seen in Figures 5.2 and 5.3.

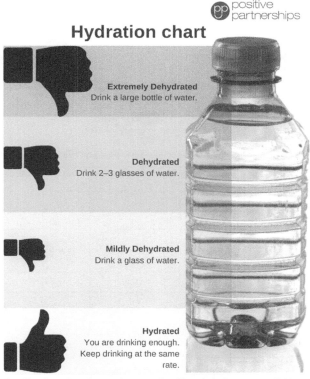

FIGURE 5.2: HYDRATION CHART
Source: Positive Partnerships

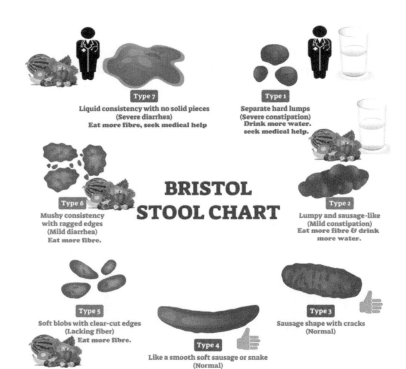

Tick the relevant number for each day of the week to share with your health professional.

Type	Monday	Tuesday	Wednesday	Thursday	Friday	Saturday	Sunday
1							
2							
3							
4							
5							
6							
7							

FIGURE 5.3: BRISTOL STOOL CHART
Source: Positive Partnerships

To learn to use a hydration chart, a child (or adult) first needs to associate the colour of their urine with the colours shown on the hydration chart. This is as simple as looking in the toilet or potty before flushing! This will only work if the toilet or potty is white; urine colours will look very different if the potty is a bright colour. Once they can match their urine colour to the chart, they then need to understand what the chart is telling them about that colour. This is where hydration charts should be selected or modified to suit your individual context.

Think about what might work best with your family. For example, a family who uses sign as a first language may have a hydration chart with signs for drink lots more water, drink a little more water, and great hydration. A family which needs more concrete (practical and realistic) information may glue water bottles to the hydration chart to illustrate how much water needs to be drunk for each colour. Other people may choose to go with a thumbs up (hydrated) or thumbs down (dehydrated, need to drink more) system. Hydration charts are not just for children – if you can smell 'wee' when you go and your urine is bright to dark yellow, you are dehydrated! Urine should be almost clear, very light in colour, and pretty much odourless. Some foods and medications can change the smell and colour of urine, so if you are unsure, check with your doctor or pharmacist.

Hydration is important for other aspects of skill development, too. It is much harder for children to toilet-train if they are not fully hydrated as their bladders are not full. When the bladder fills, the body signals are stronger and therefore easier to notice. Some children and young adults may be reluctant to drink enough water to become fully hydrated as they may be worried about having toileting 'accidents'. It is important to help them understand that urine does not smell when you are fully hydrated, but also that you should not drink way too much water as this can be unhealthy and dangerous. Technologies have also advanced in recent years, which can act as a support mechanism.

For example, period underwear or incontinence underwear has changed in the last five or so years and now looks and feels pretty much like regular underwear. This can provide the security needed for children and young people to move towards being fully hydrated while they learn to recognize their bladder signals.

TRACKING YOUR PROGRESS

While you are doing these activities, you might also like to keep a record. We have suggested a template below:

'MY INTEROCEPTION ACTIVITY RECORD'

Week X

Put a tick under each day that an interoception/mindful body awareness activity was completed.

Aim to have 2–3 ticks each day.

Activity name	Monday	Tuesday	Wednesday	Thursday	Friday	Saturday	Sunday
Finger stretch							
Toe stretch/curl							
Toe/foot walking							

CHAPTER SUMMARY

Recording and doing interoceptive activities can help you tune in to your body and its signals a little more. Developing a record of your feelings and emotions can also help you to manage your feelings and emotions, as well as helping others to understand how you might be feeling. In years gone by, there was an assumption that all people experienced feelings and emotions in the same way – for example, that all people felt/experienced hunger or even anger through exactly the same body signals. As discussed previously, we now know this not to be the case. Nummenmaa and colleagues (2014) published a 'body map' indicating where people feel emotions, which was using averages. You might therefore like to track your feelings and how they appear to you and your own 'body map'. This chapter focused on the tracking of activities and feelings; the next chapter will consider some practical strategies that you might use to manage feelings and potentially difficult emotions.

CHAPTER 6

Practical Strategies to Manage Difficult Emotions

M ANAGING EMOTIONS CAN BE DIFFICULT for all of us and will be influenced by how good we are at recognizing and accurately labelling our internal bodily signals. Sometimes being able to recognize emotions can be a positive, but as Emma shares below, this is not always the case. When Emma reflected on how her interoception has improved, she discovered that some emotions are unpleasant to experience and difficult to manage. For example, it is less pleasant being sad or angry than it is being happy. For some individuals, this is truly a revelation, and a horrible one at that. Emma was shocked by the unpleasantness of intense emotions, which had previously gone unnoticed as she moved from 'fine through big emotions into overload/ overwhelm', with no awareness until she was in or recovering from the overload. Emma found this in itself bad enough, but as she developed awareness of her difficult emotions, she found these so awful that she was getting overwhelmed in ways that seemed to her to be more frequent and more intense. Out of thousands of children, young people, and adults that Emma had been teaching and coaching in interoception, she reflected that only two other individuals had appeared to be as distressed as she was by the conscious perception of these difficult emotions.

Both they and Emma were thinking similarly when they were experiencing their emotions consciously, whether pleasant or difficult. They were using a thinking style, fairly common in autistics, that Emma calls 'broken record thinking' or 'now is forever'. What this means in practice is that whatever you are feeling at that moment, you assume you will feel it forever. So when you feel happy, you assume that you are going to be happy forever, which is lovely. However, when you feel sad, you think that sadness is going to last forever, which is awful and drives that sadness into intense distress. This leads to being over-whelmed and going into sympathetic nervous system overload.

Some of the chemical changes that occur in the brain when we are in sympathetic nervous system overload can take up to 30 minutes to reverse, which means that during those 30 minutes any stress or distress can retrigger the overload and restart the clock on the 30 minutes. When you think you are going to be significantly distressed forever, every time the brain starts to chemically calm down, that thinking kicks it back into overload. In this way, Emma and the other two individuals were stuck in a loop of chronic stress/distress for hours and sometimes days.

Emma further reflects:

> I was lucky enough to be married to a GP with qualifications and experience in mental health and psychopharmacology at the time who convinced me to talk to my GP about trialling medications to break that cycle. With medication use, I could return to calm within about an hour. A few months of this gave me confidence to shift my thinking from 'this emotion will last forever' to 'everything changes, nothing is permanent'. Once I could think like that, I was less distressed by experiencing difficult emotions and able to respond to them helpfully, rather than getting stuck in how awful they were.

Following on from this experience, Emma has learnt that teaching individuals how to respond helpfully to emotions and feelings is as important as helping them develop the skills to notice and recognize their emotions and feelings. For example, there is no point in knowing you are hot unless you know how to respond helpfully to that feeling of being hot. If you do not know how to respond helpfully to that feeling of being hot, and do nothing about it, the feeling will no doubt intensify. In time, you will be feeling very overheated and uncomfortable, but still with no idea how to cool down, which would be achieved through responding helpfully. This, in conjunction with explicitly helping the individuals to understand the impermanence of emotions and feelings, has had excellent results in terms of people being able to effectively manage and respond to difficult emotions, while avoiding the problems associated with being stuck experiencing a difficult emotion.

What this looks like in practice is good, clear, communication to scaffold and explicitly teach concepts around self-care and emotions. This can be initially quite a shift for parents and professionals who may have developed these skills without any explicit teaching. In addition, it can be difficult to understand what the reality of 'now is forever' thinking is, how this impacts people, and how hard it is to change.

CHANGING 'NOW IS FOREVER' THINKING – PRACTICAL ACTIVITIES

It sounds like a tangent but tackling 'now is forever' thinking is a critical step in improving interoception for people who have this thinking style. This can be done both explicitly and through incidental learning and modelling. For example, if we think about the weather, the weather rarely stays the same for more than a few hours, with temperatures rising and falling from dawn to dusk. Wind and rain, clouds and sunshine levels change throughout the day, with night-time weather often quite different from mid-day weather. Other practical ways to demonstrate that now is not forever use family photos or videos to show how each family member has aged and changed over the years.

Alternatively, you could do something more concrete and fun, such as making and then melting icy poles (ice lollies) or even different flavoured ice cubes. Using ice lolly moulds or an ice cube tray, pour in juice or a smoothie or water with fruit or mint or cucumber in it. Investigate and talk about what you can see, feel, and taste at this point. Then place the moulds or tray in the freezer. After a while take them out and investigate and talk about one of the cubes or lollies. Make sure to time this for when it is not quite frozen but is cold and starting to get hard. Later, remove another cube/lolly from the freezer, waiting until it is fully frozen. Compare and contrast with the earlier cubes/lollies and then leave to melt. Talk explicitly about how the items changed state, temperature, texture, etc. You can then use this example when the individual is showing signs of being stuck in that 'now is forever' thinking, by reminding them about how the lolly/cube changed with time and context.

ASSUMPTIONS ABOUT FEELINGS AND EMOTIONS

Clear communication around feelings and emotions can be difficult when people make assumptions about what others understand and how they best communicate. If, for example, you see a young person running out of the room, and when you shout stop, they don't stop, you could make a number of assumptions that may further impede conversations. Some of the possibilities are shown in the table below.

Assumption	Type of communication then used	Impact
Young person is not listening and is being rude.	Shouting loudly as the young person runs away.	Student could feel threatened or scared by the shouting, or alternatively may not hear it at all.
Young person is deaf.	Sign language or other alternative or augmentative communication (AAC) is used.	Student may be unable to respond as they don't know how to use sign language or other AAC.
Young person is scared of something.	Signal that the space is safe, or adult goes after student to ask how to help them feel safe.	Young person may be appreciative or may be confused if they were doing something like running to the toilet.

For this reason, it is important that families and professionals take the time to understand an individual and how they best communicate, and tailor their support and strategies accordingly. When an individual does not have good interoception, it is not always helpful to ask them how they are feeling, as they may not know. Nor is it useful to assume that you know exactly how they feel. Two people may express themselves in the same way and yet be feeling different emotions, just as two people may be feeling the same emotion and express this in completely different ways.

For example, some people blush when they are embarrassed, but others may blush when they are frustrated. Some people appear angry when they are anxious and so on. Instead, it is helpful to work with an individual to label or name their body signals. So you might say to an individual, 'I can see that your face and neck are red, so I can see you are blushing.' You may like to look together in a mirror so they can see the blush and try to notice what this feels like, or you could take a photo on a phone, deleting it after you have looked at it together. In this way, you are merely labelling observed events that are the manifestation of internal body signals.

Think about how you use these descriptions, though. 'I can see that tears are running down your face' is a very different piece of information to 'I think you are sad'. This is important, because it can be confusing to be told how you feel when you aren't actually feeling that emotion. For example, we often cry when we observe acts of kindness or compassion – we may not be sad at all, but moved. Emma recalls a young lady she worked with who thought that when people cried, it indicated that they were just starting to become sad as that was how tears had been labelled for her. Over time, as individuals build up a greater connection to their internal and external body signals, they will be able to notice collections of signals and these can be explored to find the right label for their particular experience. This can take time and patience and be an ongoing process.

Indeed, the process can take several years for individuals to recognize and understand signals from their bodies. For example, Emma reflects on her experiences of grief.

I have only just discovered that one of my internal body signals around grief is a pain in my neck/throat area that feels as if I have a fist pushing outwards from inside my neck. However, until I worked this out with the help of a counsellor, I thought I was having a recurrence of thyroid issues! Grief is an intense and very difficult emotion to manage and yet it is one that most people will experience at least once in their life, if not many more times at different levels of intensity. In my grief journey, I found it important to rely on external prompts to manage gaps in my interoception. As an example, I cried a lot during my initial period of intense grief, which dehydrated me, which led to headaches. I did not realize I was dehydrated until I went back to using my hydration charts, which helped me to manage my water intake to increase my hydration levels. As my

> headaches became less frequent, I could minimize my fear: not only was my thyroid problem not recurring, but I was also not having some major problem with my head.

This example neatly captures something that non-autistic people might not have realized about those of us on the autism spectrum. We cannot always make sense of things because we can forget to take context into account or we either over- or under-generalize experiences and events. Emma's neck/throat was uncomfortable when her thyroid was needing to be removed, so she over-generalized that every time her neck/throat felt uncomfortable she had thyroid issues. This was despite her thyroid had been surgically removed and therefore could not be the source of the issue.

MANAGING YOUR FEELINGS BY TUNING IN TO YOUR FEELINGS

Feelings can be as challenging as emotions for some people, particularly those with sensory sensitivities, such as autistic people. When a feeling is challenging or uncomfortable and it is not helpfully addressed, it can become unbearable and lead to emotional overload. Imagine if you could feel the hairs growing through your skin after you shaved, and this feeling was uncomfortable. If you did not address this feeling, it could become significantly distressing. Trying to explain to someone that your hairs are bothering you can lead to an assumption of psychosis or other mental illness, as it is rare for non-autistic people to notice the hairs growing through their skin, let alone in such detail.

Interestingly, individuals can have highly sensitive interoception for some internal body signals, whether these are pleasant, unpleasant, or neutral, while not being tuned in at all to other internal body signals. This is why an individual may be unable to tell when they need to go to the toilet, for example, but be acutely aware of their body temperature. Everyone is different, and a person's interoceptive profile is as complex as a wider sensory profile. Even once that complexity has been taken into account, a person's ability to sit with uncomfortable or difficult feelings and emotions is also highly individual.

No matter how comfortable with the uncomfortable an individual may be, this is likely to be impacted by contextual factors. A young person who is OK with being tired all the time due to chronic insomnia may be less able to experience those feelings comfortably if they have additional stressors, such as an exam or a first date, or a highly stressful sensory experience. To illustrate this in a way that is easier to relate to for people who are able to self-manage and self-regulate unaided most of the time, it is useful to think about a trip to the supermarket. If you are driving to the supermarket and you are healthy, well rested, and have just eaten a nice, enjoyable meal, then you are much less likely to experience road rage. If, however, you are tired, unwell, and hungry, when a car narrowly misses hitting you due to that driver's carelessness, you are far more likely to not be comfortable with the experience and instead to feel and/or express road rage.

HELPING OTHERS TO RECOGNIZE FEELINGS AND EMOTIONS

When we can be comfortable with the uncomfortable, it provides us with a bigger window in which to helpfully manage or address the uncomfortable feeling or emotion. Strategies can be used that support the development of being comfortable with the uncomfortable, including modelling, explicit teaching, and clear information about the 'what' and 'why' of the feeling or emotion. Take, for example, hunger, which is generally considered to be uncomfortable. Some people are very comfortable with the uncomfortableness of hunger. They sense the signals and plan what to eat when. Other people cannot stand feeling hungry and need to eat instantly or they become agitated or 'hangry'. If you care for or work with an individual who frequently becomes hangry, it helps to know if they are consciously aware of their hunger prior to being hangry or if they had no idea that they were feeling hungry until the sensation was overwhelmingly uncomfortable. Either way, individuals can be helped to understand the benefit of eating a healthy snack should they consciously feel their hunger developing or feel their extreme level of hunger and nothing less.

We have, of course, all experienced being hangry, but usually we can recognize the signals and act accordingly. Emma reflects on some of the strategies that she has developed that help her to manage to accurately locate and identify bodily feelings and their impact on felt emotions.

I am one of many people who usually carries a healthy snack with me, to prevent or minimize the hangry experience. I have learnt over time that as soon as my mind wanders to the snack, I need to eat it all; otherwise, I am likely to end up hangry and yet uncertain how I arrived there. I am currently working on a proactive anxiety strategy as I am unaware when I am becoming anxious, and as a result can end up in a state that people usually interpret as angry but is in fact quite advanced anxiety. I was much more comfortable with those same uncomfortable feelings of advanced anxiety before they were labelled for me in ways that made me think they were negative states that indicated some defect or deficit.

Again, some level of being comfortable with the uncomfortable, of 'being friends with' or accepting as valid and valuable one's whole range of feelings and emotions, without judging them as being good or bad, is very helpful. When helping individuals to recognize and respond to difficult emotions in other people, it is helpful to use similar strategies to those listed already in this chapter. For example, if you are feeling upset, it is more useful to describe your internal body signals and how you would like to be responded to. For example, 'I am upset at the moment. Can you see how my shoulders are leaning forward and my head is down a bit? My chest also feels heavy and my voice is a bit quieter. When I am upset, I like someone to make me a cup of tea or offer me some biscuits.' Providing external context cues that help you to recognize your emotions can also scaffold the development of confidence in others in their own understanding and responding to their own and others' emotions.

This is where things get even more complicated. What if we are better at recognizing difficult emotions and feelings in other people than in ourselves? The impact of someone recognizing difficulties in others when they don't recognize it within themselves can be exhausting for an individual, as Emma recollects below.

> I cannot recognize when I am exhausted, but I can usually tell when other people are, especially if I know them. My own exhaustion is easy to cope with: because I don't notice or recognize it, I don't need to cope with it! Although, obviously, this results in me getting so exhausted that I am unable to do anything at all for 24–48 hours on a fairly regular basis. However, I do not find that experience difficult or challenging either and love my 'pyjama weekends' where I just hang out on the couch or in bed all weekend. In contrast, I can find other people's exhaustion challenging, and if they are not open to doing something helpful about their need to rest, I can find this quite distressing.

When supporting children, young people, and adults to learn how to recognize and respond helpfully to the emotions of others, it is important not to assume that their skills in relation to others are the same as skills in regard to their own emotions and feelings. Also, think about the difference between learning a skill for the sake of learning it and learning a skill that can be useful across contexts throughout life. Finally, we need to reflect on what we can and can't do to help others. As adults, other people's emotions are not actually our own individual responsibility. Yes, we should be kind and caring, and it is nice to respond helpfully to others and their emotions, but it is not our responsibility to ensure they are happy or feel better. However, what we should be striving for as parents, carers, and professionals is to work with children and young people in ways that model and emphasize kindness and compassion. So when an autistic student cries because another student in their class is crying, this is approached with the kindness and compassion that lies behind the autistic student's tears. They are distressed that someone else is distressed, even if they cannot articulate this or respond in any other way.

Recently, Emma was asked if she knew that she was a rescuer. Much of her need to save others comes from her strong sense of social justice, but there is a large chunk that comes from being taught to use the phrases 'How can I help?' or 'What can I do to help?' as acceptable or suitable phrases to use when encountering people who are upset, distressed, angry, or demonstrating any other difficult emotion. Being taught these phrases, as a person who understands language literally, Emma thought she was meant to help everyone, that she was responsible for fixing everything, for restoring them to happiness. It is only with age and experience and explicit prompting that Emma has come to realize that she is not responsible for everyone she comes into contact with in this way.

Imagine as a five-year-old thinking you are responsible for

the happiness or well-being of everyone in your class, no matter what the circumstances! You can understand how tiring this would be at the very least, and how, at its worst, this could provoke severe anxiety. We are not suggesting that people have no part to play in restoring the emotions of others to equilibrium, but we are saying that when children, young people, and adults feel they are totally responsible, it can be very unhelpful in the long run. Instead, it is important to teach helpful skills at the same time as self-care skills.

THE IMPORTANCE OF SELF-CARE

As adults, we know that it is important to look after ourselves first, as we cannot look after others in the long term unless we take care of ourselves. Using Christine Misernadino's spoon theory terminology, which is popular in the autistic community, 'you can't help others if you have run out of spoons' (Misernadino, 2003). Another analogy is that if you keep letting people take water from your well, but you don't replenish your water, you will eventually run out of water. For autistic young people and adults, this can result in what we term autistic burnout. Autistic burnout is not an official diagnosis from any profession; it is a community name for a state of being where an autistic person is barely able to function, or completely unable to function, due to being required to behave in ways that are not natural to them and/or being overwhelmed by the environment and the people in it for a period of time that is unsustainable.

The anecdotally high rates of autistic burnout in adolescence and adult years indicate that this is an area for further research, and also that autistic people are not always aware when they are headed down that path and/or do not know what to do about it. This seems to be the sadly logical conclusion of not knowing how to respond helpfully to our own and others' difficult emotions.

A slightly different but perhaps more recognizable scenario for parents is the end of the school day: either on the way home or as soon as arriving home, the child 'loses it' and gets highly emotional, distressed, or otherwise dysregulated. Often the child has actually had a really good day at school, according to their teacher and/or the child themselves. However, the effort it has taken the child to have that good day was so emotionally challenging that they are unable to keep it all together any longer once they have left school.

In order to prevent this damaging cycle, it is helpful to set up more healthy coping patterns, including acknowledging and demonstrating that all people need help dealing with difficult emotions at some point in their life, and that asking for and/ or accepting help is both healthy and useful. Demonstrating the need to ask for help can start with practical things, such as asking for help unpacking groceries and putting them away. However, it needs to encompass asking for and accepting support in managing emotions.

An example of this is when a parent says to their child, 'I am feeling a bit upset today. Would it be OK for you to give me a hug? When you hug me, it helps to know that I won't be sad forever.' Or if a child hates hugging but likes music: 'I am feeling a bit upset today. Could you play me a song on your phone? Your music helps me to know that there are happy things in the world.' In addition, if a child asks if their parent is sad, it is important, if the parent is sad, to acknowledge the feeling, say what could help and why, and/or accept help offered by the child, without making the child feel responsible for the parent's emotional state.

PRACTICAL STRATEGIES: REVISITING THE HAND MODEL OF THE BRAIN

When feeling tired, stressed, anxious, or any other difficult emotion, parents and professionals both need to demonstrate that experiencing these emotions is a normal part of human existence, by stating how they feel. They need to talk about healthy strategies to manage these difficult emotions helpfully. Emma still recalls how relieved she was when she moved somewhere where taking short breaks or 'nana naps' was socially acceptable and widely talked about. If she was socially exhausted, she felt comfortable saying that she needed to go home and have a nana nap, even though she had no intention of sleeping, but was merely needing alone time.

If children and young people are encouraged to take the kinds of breaks that work for them when they need them, this will prevent things like autistic burnout. However, we are all different and not all autistics want silent alone time in a darkened room. Some will benefit from physical activities such as running, bouncing on a trampoline, swinging, skipping, swimming, or boxing. Others may like to read, draw, paint, and/or listen to music of their choosing.

Another practical strategy is to teach individuals Dan Siegel's (2010) 'hand model of the brain', which helps develop awareness that it is not a 'character defect' to exhibit survival behaviours of flop, drop, freeze, flight, or fight when feeling overwhelmed, but rather these behaviours occur a result of the way the brain works. This model can be used to support solution-seeking rather than blaming self or others. In this model, the three main parts of the brain involved in behaviour – the reptile/survival brain, the limbic/emotional brain, and the neocortex/thinking cap of the brain – are used to demonstrate how emotions and feelings impact behaviour. In this model, the mindfulness part of the brain is a sub-section of the thinking cap of the brain, which is active when the fist is fully closed and the middle fingertips are touching the palm of the hand, as shown in Figure 6.1, below.

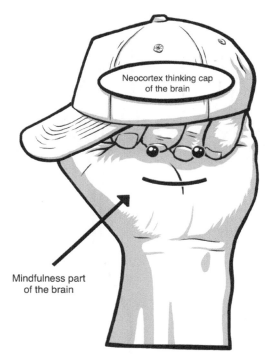

FIGURE 6.1: THE THINKING CAP – ADAPTED FROM DAN
SIEGEL'S (2010) HAND MODEL OF THE BRAIN

In this model, when your fist is closed with your thumb under the fingers, your neocortex or the thinking cap of the brain is in control. This is when you can learn, be engaged in the moment, make choices, and control your behaviour and emotions. As your fingers lift up, the thinking cap falls off, and the neocortex is no longer in control. Now your limbic brain – your emotional brain – is in control. You may be expressing and experiencing 'big emotions'. When your emotions are in control, it is very hard to manage your behaviours as your emotions are controlling you – you are not in control of them. This is 'flipping your lid, as shown in Figure 6.2, below'.

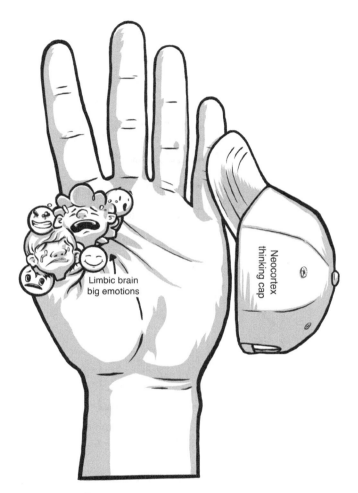

Limbic brain
big emotions

Neocortex
thinking cap

FIGURE 6.2: FLIPPING YOUR LID – ADAPTED FROM DAN
SIEGEL'S (2010) HAND MODEL OF THE BRAIN

What can happen next is that the brain moves into survival instinct, which is when the most ancient part of your brain takes control – the reptile brain. This is represented by the open palm of the hand. When your reptile brain is in control, you cannot make conscious choices. Your survival instinct is controlling you. This is 'overload' or 'meltdown' or 'losing it'. What we need to achieve is shown in Figure 6.3.

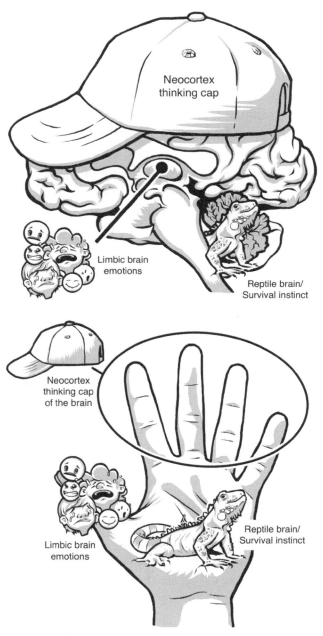

FIGURE 6.3: STRIVING FOR BALANCE – ADAPTED FROM
DAN SIEGEL'S (2010) HAND MODEL OF THE BRAIN

In the hand model of the brain, your fingers and thumb open and close in response to your internal body signals and your interpretation of the world around you. Bodily stress and distress, anxiety, and fear make the fingers and thumb open up. Bodily safety, contentment, and calm make the fingers and thumb close again.

When the fist is fully closed around the thumb, the mindfulness part of the brain is connected and can be used. This is represented by the middle two fingernails. Engaging in mindful body awareness – that is to say, interoception activities – brings the thinking cap of the brain back down and activates it. This does not work during survival mode as the brain prioritizes survival. Another way to look at this is using a scale of 0–100, where 100 is survival mode, 99 is big emotions, and in 0–98 the thinking cap of the brain is connected.

Lastly, doing interoception activities when you are at 99 or less, particularly at 98 or less on a scale of 100, is a highly effective way to manage difficult emotions as you neurologically and biologically calm down as well as break the cycle of 'now is forever' thinking by solely focusing on internal body signals (see Figure 6.4). Emma's adult clients report the same kind of effect as the children and young people in her research on interoception.

> I did the hand stretch interoception when I was starting to get really anxious and it calmed me down enough that I didn't need to leave the event. (Julie, autistic adult)

> When I am so stressed that I can't talk, if I do a few minutes of interoception, I can talk again. This has changed my life. (Zaph, autistic adult)

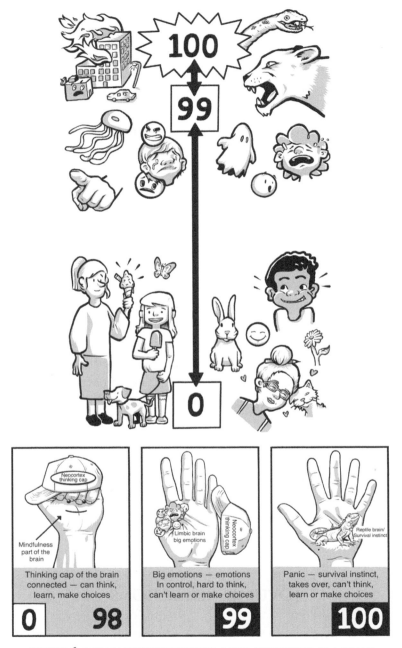

FIGURE 6.4: ENGAGING IN MINDFUL BODY AWARENESS AS A SCALE

These activities are included in Chapter 5. Particularly check out the 'belly breathing', which is also known as diaphragmatic breathing. In this interoception activity, you focus on feeling the rise and fall of your belly as you breathe in through your nose deeply and out through your mouth. If you are not used to deep breathing, this can be hard to do, so you can place your hands with fingertips just touching over your abdomen during the activity. As you breathe in, the fingertips should move apart, and as you breathe out, they should slightly overlap. Belly breathing can be done sitting, standing, or lying down – give it a try.

CHAPTER SUMMARY

What we have learnt from this chapter is that while it is important to help others and use strategies to enable others to better recognize their own feelings, we do also need to take care of ourselves – if we are not well looked after, we will be of little help to others. When we are helping others to recognize and decode their feelings, practical examples are important in helpfully translating what can be complex signals that our bodies are giving us. We have seen from Emma's personal reflections and those of others that accurately interpreting signals is not always easy! The final section below will seek to bring together the key ideas that we have touched on throughout the book and suggest some practical strategies that you might draw on both for engaging with your own body and helping others to manage theirs.

OVERALL REFLECTIONS

Both research and more anecdotal reports have consistently indicated that teaching children and young people to notice their internal body signals through short activities focused on prompting them to notice changes in body state does facilitate the development or improvement of interoceptive awareness. As research by Emma has shown, the effects of these interventions can be crucial in their impacts on the reduction of behavioural incidences within schools and visible increases in engagement with learning. Children and young people tend to enjoy doing the interoception activities as they teach them to connect both with themselves and others. Such alternative ways of engaging with children and young people may lead to effectively setting them up for the best possible outcomes in managing self-regulation. The activities are not onerous and can be completed in short bursts throughout the day.

To end this book, we would like to share our top tips for supporting the people you care for:

- Engage with your young people at a level that makes sense to them – explicitly label emotions and feelings to help scaffold their own understandings of their internal states.
- Remember you are not responsible for other people's emotions – you can support these but not control them. You need to provide the necessary tools to support people doing that for themselves.
- Interoceptive abilities (or lack thereof) are not 'good' or 'bad'. It is not an individual's fault that they are not in tune with their own body's signals. They may, however, need support to recognize and work with these.
- Make sure you find time to look after yourself. You need to be in tune with your own bodily signals and recognize when you need rest or support if you are going to be helpful in supporting others.

References

Aguiar, W. & Halseth, R. (2015) *Aboriginal Peoples and Historic Trauma: The Processes of Intergenerational Transmission*. Prince George, BC: National Collaborating Centre for Aboriginal Health/Centre de collaboration nationale de la santé autochtone.

Ahissar, M., Nahum, M., Nelken, I., & Hochstein, S. (2009) 'Reverse hierarchies and sensory learning.' *Philosophical Transactions of the Royal Society B 364*, 1515. https://doi.org/10.1098/rstb.2008.0253

Badoud, D. & Tsakiris, M. (2017) 'From the body's viscera to the body's image: Is there a link between interoception and body image concerns?' *Neuroscience & Biobehavioural Reviews 77*, 237–246. https://doi.org/10.1016/j.neubiorev.2017.03.017

Balzarotti, S., Biassoni, F., Villani, D., Prunas, A., & Velotti, P. (2016) 'Individual differences in cognitive emotion regulation: Implications for subjective and psychological well-being.' *Journal of Happiness Studies 17*, 125–143. https://doi.org/10.1007/s10902-014-9587-3

Berriman, J., Stevenson, R.J., Thayer, Z.C., Thompson, E., *et al.* (2016) 'Testing the importance of the medial temporal lobes in human interoception: Does it matter if there is a memory component to the task?' *Neuropsychologia 91*, 371–379. https://doi.org/10.1016/j.neuropsychologia.2016.09.005

Blair, C. & Raver, C.C. (2015) 'School readiness and self-regulation: A developmental psychobiological approach.' *Annual Review of Psychology 66*, 711–731. https://doi.org/10.1146/annurev-psych-010814-015221

Brewer, R., Cook, R., & Bird, G. (2016) 'Alexithymia: A general deficit of interoception.' *Royal Society Open Science 3*, 10. https://doi.org/10.1098/rsos.150664

Calì, G., Ambrosini, E., Picconi, L., & Mehling, W. (2015) 'Investigating the relationship between interoceptive accuracy, interoceptive awareness, and emotional susceptibility.' *Frontiers in Psychology*. https://doi.org/10.3389/fpsyg.2015.01202

Cook-Cottone, C.P. (2015) *Mindfulness and Yoga for Self-Regulation: A Primer for Mental Health Professionals*. New York, NY: Springer Publishing Company.

Couto, B., Adolfi, F., Sedeno, L., Salles, A., *et al.* (2015) 'Disentangling interoception: Insights from focal strokes affecting the perception of external and internal milieus.' *Frontiers in Psychology*. https://doi.org/10.3389/fpsyg.2015.00503

Craig, A.D. (2002) 'How do you feel? Interoception: The sense of the physiological condition of the body.' *Nature Reviews Neuroscience 3*, 8, 655–666. https://doi.org/10.1038/nrn894

Craig, A.D. (2003) 'Interoception: The sense of the physiological condition of the body.' *Current Opinion in Neurobiology 13*, 4, 500–505. https://doi.org/10.1016/S0959-4388(03)00090-4

Craig, A.D. (2007) 'Interoception and Emotion: A Neuroanatomical Perspective.' In M. Lewis, J.M. Haviland-Jones, & L. Feldman Barrett (eds) *Handbook of Emotions*. New York, NY: Guilford Press.

Craig, A.D. (2009) 'How do you feel – now? The anterior insula and human awareness.' *Nature Reviews Neuroscience 10*, 1, 59–70. https://doi.org/10.1038/nrn2555

Damasio, A. (1999) *Feeling of What Happens: Body and Emotion in the Making of Consciousness*. New York, NY: Houghton Mifflin Harcourt.

Damasio, A. & Carvalho, G.B. (2013) 'The nature of feelings: Evolutionary and neurobiological origins.' *Nature Reviews Neuroscience 14*, 143–152. https://doi.org/10.1038/nrn3403

DuBois, D., Ameis, S.H., Lai, M.-C., Casanova, M.F., & Desarkar, P. (2016) 'Interoception in autism spectrum disorder: A review.' *International Journal of Developmental Neuroscience 52*, 104–111. https://doi.org/10.1016/j.ijdevneu.2016.05.001

Durie, M. (n.d.) 'Te Whare Tapa Whā, Maori health model.' Ministry of Health/Manatū Hauora. www.health.govt.nz/our-work/populations/maori-health/maori-health-models/maori-health-models-te-whare-tapa-wha

Evans, G.W. & Kim, P. (2013) 'Childhood poverty, chronic stress, self-regulation, and coping.' *Child Development Perspectives 7*, 1, 43–48.

Fiene, L. (2018) 'Exploring interoception in autism: A mixed-methods design for understanding autistic experiences.' Unpublished doctoral dissertation, University of Southern Queensland, Australia.

Fiene, L., Ireland, M., & Brownlow, C. (2018) 'The Interoception Sensory Questionnaire (ISQ): A scale to measure interoceptive challenges in adults.' *Journal of Autism and Developmental Disorders 48*, 3354–3366. https://doi.org/10.1007/s10803-018-3600-3

Flook, L., Goldberg, S.B., Pinger, L.J., & Davidson, R.J. (2015) 'Promoting prosocial behavior and self-regulatory skills in preschool children through a mindfulness-based kindness curriculum. *Developmental Psychology 51*, 1, 44–51. https://dx.doi.org/10.1037/a0038256

Fotopoulou, A. & Tsakiris, M. (2017) 'Mentalizing homeostasis: The social origins of interoceptive inference.' *Neuropsychoanalysis. An Interdisciplinary Journal for Psychoanalysis and the Neurosciences 19*, 1, 3–28. https://doi.org/10.1080/15294145.2017.1294031

Fox Lee, S. (2019) 'Psychology's own mindfulness: Ellen Langer and the social politics of scientific interest in "active noticing".' *Journal of the History of the Behavioral Sciences 55*, 3, 216–229. https://doi.org/10.1002/jhbs.21975

Furman, D.J., Waugh, C.E., Bhattacharjee, K., Thompson, R.J., & Gotlib, I.H. (2013) 'Interoceptive awareness, positive affect, and decision making in major depressive disorder.' *Journal of Affective Disorders 151*, 2, 780–785. https://doi.org/10.1016/j.jad.2013.06.044

Füstös, J., Gramann, K., Herbert, B.M., & Pollatos, O. (2012) 'On the embodiment of emotion regulation: Interoceptive awareness facilitates reappraisal.' *Social Cognitive and Affective Neuroscience 8*, 8, 911–917. https://doi.org/10.1093/scan/nss089

Garfinkel, S.N., Tiley, C., O'Keefe, S., Harrison, N.A., Seth, A.K., & Critchley, H.D. (2016) 'Discrepancies between dimensions of interoception in autism: Implications for emotion and anxiety.' *Biological Psychology 114*, 117–126. https://doi.org/10.1016/j.biopsycho.2015.12.003

Goleman, D. (1995) *Emotional Intelligence: Why It Can Matter More Than IQ*. New York, NY: Bantam Books.

Goodall, E. (2019) *Helping Children Understand and Express Emotions: A Practical Interoception Activity Book*. Adelaide: Healthy Possibilities.

Goodall, E., Lean, C., Leslie, M., Goodall, E., McCauley, M., & Heays, D. (2019) *Interoception 201 Activity Guide*. Adelaide: Department for Education, South Australia.

Goodall, E. (2020) 'Interoception as a proactive tool to decrease challenging behaviour.' *Scan: The Journal for Educators 39*, 1, 20–24.

Goodall, E. (2021) 'Facilitating interoceptive awareness as a self-management and self-regulation tool to increase engagement in learning and education.' Unpublished master's dissertation, University of Southern Queensland, Australia.

Grecucci, A., Koch, I., & Rumiati, R.I. (2011) 'The role of emotional context in facilitating imitative actions.' *Acta Psychologica 138*, 2, 311–315. https://doi.org/10.1016/j.actpsy.2011.07.005

Gross, J.J. & Thompson, R.A. (2007) 'Emotion Regulation: Conceptual Foundations.' In J.J. Gross (ed.) *Handbook of Emotion Regulation.* New York, NY: Guilford Press.

Heatherton, T.F. & Tice, D.M. (1994) *Losing Control: How and Why People Fail at Self-Regulation.* San Diego, CA: Academic Press.

Idusohan-Moizer, H., Sawicka, A., Dendle, J., & Albany, M. (2015) 'Mindfulness-based cognitive therapy for adults with intellectual disabilities: An evaluation of the effectiveness of mindfulness in reducing symptoms of depression and anxiety.' *Journal of Intellectual Disability Research 59*, 2, 93–104. https://doi.org/10.1111/jir.12082

Kanbara, K. & Fukunaga, M. (2016) 'Links among emotional awareness, somatic awareness and autonomic homeostatic processing.' *BioPsychoSocial Medicine 10*, 1, 16. https://doi.org/10.1186/s13030-016-0059-3

Khoury, N.M., Lutz, J., & Schuman-Olivier, Z. (2018) 'Interoception in psychiatric disorders: A review of randomized, controlled trials with interoception-based interventions.' *Harvard Review of Psychiatry 26*, 5, 250–263. https://doi.org/10.1097/HRP.0000000000000170

Lynch, S.A. & Simpson, C.G. (2004) 'Sensory processing: Meeting individual needs using the seven senses.' *Young Exceptional Children 7*, 4, 2–9. https://doi.org/10.1177%2F109625060400700401

Mahler, K. (2016) *Interoception: The Eighth Sensory System.* Overland Park, KS: AAPC Publishing.

Meessen, J., Mainz, V., Gauggel, S., Volz-Sidiropoulou, E., Sütterlin, S., & Forkmann, T. (2016) 'The relationship between interoception and metacognition: A pilot study.' *Journal of Psychophysiology 30*, 2, 76–86. https://doi.org/10.1027/0269-8803/a000157

Michalski, C.A., Diemert, L.M., Helliwell, J.F., Goel, V., & Rosella, L.C. (2020) 'Relationship between sense of community belonging and self-rated health across life stages.' *SSM Population Health 12*, 100676. https://doi.org/10.1016/j.ssmph.2020.100676

Miserandino, C. (2003) 'The Spoon Theory.' But You Don't Look Sick. https://butyoudontlooksick.com/articles/written-by-christine/the-spoon-theory

Moffitt, T.E., Poulton, R., & Caspi, A. (2013) 'Lifelong impact of early self-control.' *American Scientist 101*, 352–359. www.researchgate.net/publication/275701883_Lifelong_Impact_of_Early_Self-Control

Moses, L.J. & Baird, J.A. (1999) 'Metacognition.' In R.A. Wilson & F.C. Keil (eds) *The MIT Encyclopaedia of the Cognitive Sciences*. Cambridge, MA: MIT Press.

Mul, C.-l., Stagg, S.D., Herbelin, B., & Aspell, J.E. (2018) 'The feeling of me feeling for you: Interoception, alexithymia and empathy in autism.' *Journal of Autism and Developmental Disorders 48*, 2953–2967. https://doi.org/10.1007/s10803-018-3564-3

Murphy, J., Brewer, R., Catmur, C., & Bird, G. (2017) 'Interoception and psychopathology: A developmental neuroscience perspective.' *Developmental Cognitive Neuroscience 23*, 45–56. https://doi.org/10.1016/j.dcn.2016.12.006

Nathan, P. (2019) 'Creating a Safe Supportive Environment (CASSE): A Psychodynamically-Informed Community Intervention for Aboriginal Communities in Central Australia.' In D. Kealy & J.S. Ogrodniczuk (eds) *Contemporary Psychodynamic Psychotherapy: Evolving Clinical Practice*. Academic Press. https://doi.org/10.1016/B978-0-12-813373-6.00025-8

Nigg, J.T. (2017) 'Annual Research Review: On the relations among self-regulation, self-control, executive functioning, effortful control, cognitive control, impulsivity, risk-taking, and inhibition for developmental psychopathology.' *Journal of Child Psychology and Psychiatry 58*, 4, 361–383. https://doi.org/10.1111/jcpp.12675

Nummenmaa, L., Glerean, E., Hari, R., & Hietanen, J.K. (2014) 'Bodily maps of emotions.' *Proceedings of the National Academy of Sciences of the United States of America 111*, 2, 646–651. https://doi.org/10.1073/pnas.1321664111

Oldroyd, K., Pasupathi, M., & Wainryb, C. (2019) 'Social antecedents to the development of interoception: Attachment related processes are associated with interoception.' *Frontiers in Psychology 10*, 712. https://doi.org/10.3389/fpsyg.2019.00712

Pascoe, M. & Crewther, S.G. (2017) 'A systematic review of randomised control trials examining the effects of mindfulness on stress and anxious symptomatology.' *Psychoneuroendocrinology 86*, 152–168. https://doi.org/10.1016/j.psyneuen.2017.08.008

Paulus, M.P. & Stein, M.B. (2010) 'Interoception in anxiety and depression.' *Brain Structure and Function 214*, 451–463. https://doi.org/10.1007/s00429-010-0258-9

Porges, S. (2004) 'Neuroception: A subconscious system for detecting threats and safety.' *Semantic Scholar.* www.semanticscholar.org/paper/NEUROCEPTION%3A-A-Subconscious-System-for-Detecting-Porges/7aa83dc8d507fc38aa97e22233d96fd878f f7e51

Pulotu-Endemann, F.K. (2007) *A Pacific Model of Health: The Fonofale Model.* Ministry of Health/Manatū Hauora. https://www.health.govt.nz/system/files/documents/publications/improving-quality-of-care-for-pacific-peoples-may08.pdf

Schaan, V.K., Schultz, A., Rubel, J.A., Bernstein, M., Domes, G., Schachinger, H., & Vogele, C. (2019) 'Childhood trauma affects stress-related interoceptive accuracy.' *Frontiers in Psychiatry 10*, 750. https://doi.org/10.3389/fpsyt.2019.00750

Schauder, K.B., Mash, L.E., Bryant, L.K., & Cascio, C.J. (2015) 'Interoceptive ability and body awareness in autism spectrum disorder.' *Journal of Experimental Child Psychology 131*, 193–200. https://doi.org/10.1016/j.jecp.2014.11.002

Sher, M.L. (2016) 'How getting a lot done can get in the way of major success.' *Canadian Manager 41*, 1, 29–31.

Shields, A.M., Cicchetti, D., & Ryan, R.M. (1994) 'The development of emotional and behavioral self-regulation and social competence among maltreated school-age children.' *Development and Psychopathology 6*, 1, 57–75. https://doi.org/10.1017/S0954579400005885

Siegel, D.J. (2010) *Mindsight: The New Science of Personal Transformation.* New York, NY: Bantam Dell Publishing.

Slutske, W.S., Moffitt, T.E., Poulton, R., & Caspi, A. (2012) 'Uncontrolled temperament at age 3 predicts disordered gambling at age 32: A longitudinal study of a complete birth cohort.' *Psychological Science 23*, 5, 510–516. https://doi.org/10.1177/0956797611429708

van der Kolk, B.A. (2014) *The Body Keeps the Score: Brain, Mind, and Body in the Healing of Trauma.* New York, NY: Viking.

Vogel, S. & Schwabe, L. (2016) 'Learning and memory under stress: Implications for the classroom.' *Nature Partner Journals: Science of Learning 1*, 16011. https://doi.org/10.1038/npjscilearn.2016.11

Wellman, H.M. (1985) 'The Child's Theory of Mind: The Development of Conceptions of Cognition.' In S.R. Yussen (ed.) *The Growth of Reflection in Children.* New York, NY: Academic Press.

Wilutzky, W. (2015) 'Emotions as pragmatic and epistemic actions.' *Frontiers in Psychology 6.* https://doi.org/10.3389/fpsyg.2015.01593

Yehuda, R., Daskalakis, N.P., Bierer, L.M., Bader, H.N., *et al.* (2016) 'Holocaust exposure induced intergenerational effects on FKBP5 methylation.' *Biological Psychiatry 80,* 5, 372–380.

Zamariola, G., Frost, N., Van Oost, A., Corneille, O., & Luminet, O. (2019) 'Relationship between interoception and emotion regulation: New evidence from mixed methods (report).' *Journal of Affective Disorders 246,* 480–485. https://doi.org/10.1016/j.jad.2018.12.101

Zitron, L. & Gao, Y. (2017) 'The Effects of Mindfulness-Based Interventions on Physiological Regulation.' In M. Powietrzyńska & K. Tobin (eds) *Weaving Complementary Knowledge Systems and Mindfulness to Educate a Literate Citizenry for Sustainable and Healthy Lives.* Leiden: Brill Sense.

Index